CHINA AS A RISING WORLD POWER
AND ITS RESPONSE TO 'GLOBALIZATION'

Discourse is a fundamental component of policymaking in democratic political systems, but when and how does it matter at times of major political institutional change? Moreover, what is the power of Europeanization in the domestic and international arenas with regard to policy change? This book provides enlightening answers to these questions by considering policy discourse, Europeanization, and the classic variables of politics in their institutional context. If offers sophisticated theoretical analysis grounded in empirically-rich comparative case studies on security and defence coopera- tion, international negotiations on trade and agricultural policy, deregulation of telecommunications and banking, and reform of anti-discrimination policy.

This was first published as a special issue of *The Review of International Affairs*.

Ronald C. Keith is a Professor of Political Science at the University of Calgary.

CHINA AS A RISING WORLD POWER AND ITS RESPONSE TO 'GLOBALIZATION'

Edited by Ronald C. Keith

Routledge
Taylor & Francis Group

LONDON AND NEW YORK

First published 2005
by Routledge
4 Park Square, Milton Park, Abingdon, Oxon OX14 4RN
605 Third Avenue, New York, NY 10017

Routledge is an imprint of the Taylor & Francis Group, an informa business

© 2005 Ronald C. Keith

Typeset in Times New Roman by Elite Typesetting Techniques Ltd,
Eastleigh, Hampshire, UK

British Library Cataloguing in Publication Data
A catalogue record for this book is available
from the British Library

Library of Congress Cataloguing in Publication Data

ISBN13: 978-0-415-34825-6 (hbk)
ISBN13: 978-0-415-46417-8 (pbk)

Contents

China as a Rising World Power and its Response to 'Globalization'

RONALD C. KEITH

The People's Republic of China (PRC) is the first developing state to become a world power. As a new world power the PRC has a particular perspective on 'globalization' and its impact on state sovereignty in world politics. The PRC professes a qualified, but, nonetheless, 'revisionist' pragmatism on the relations between states in the developing context of interdependence. Chinese foreign policy has espoused a new 'idealist' view on multilateralism and multipolarity while at the same time demonstrating a cautious approach to the realities of the balance of power. It sees globalization, particularly economic globalization as inevitable, and yet it still pits the equality of state sovereignty, against 'hegemony', unipolarity and unilateralism.

Chinese foreign policy rejects the deliberate exaggeration of declining state sovereignty in the face of globalization and alternatively suggests the state's innovative capacity to adapt to basic changes in international conditions over time. On the other hand, the longstanding emphasis on China's 'independent foreign policy' (*duli zizhu waiguan zhengce*) has had to be updated so as to insure a more balanced and rational approach to globalization. In sum, the

Dr. Ronald C. Keith is currently Professor of the Department of Political Science at the University of Calgary, Alberta, Canada. Related research assistance was provided by Xu Kai. The University of Calgary provided research funding.

PRC has adjusted the underlying rationality of its foreign policy so as to take advantage of the new global opportunities of trade, investment and technological cooperation while seeking to influence the rules of international organization and regimes so as to insure their qualification in relation to the priorities of China's own national economic development.

One might argue that Chinese foreign policy has, at least in formal terms, adapted rather well to the complexities of the state system in its response to globalization, and that this is all the more remarkable in that history did not offer the PRC much respite in this regard. Achieving such status has, however, involved extraordinary tuition as well as very interesting self-study of the changing implications of China's adaptation to the vicissitudes of colonialism, imperialism, neocolonialism and now economic globalization. In fact, the protracted delay in the recognition of China's status as a world power no doubt continues in part to service Chinese revisionism in its cautious adaptation to globalization.

The historical context of Cold War containment and non-recognition is well known. The Chinese response to this context was to place a special, if not too exclusive emphasis on the PRC's own jealously guarded national sovereignty. Moreover, the PRC had had to contend with hostile alliances and bilateral security arrangements, and its experience with multilateralism was, therefore, episodic. With the notable exception of its connections with the non-aligned movement, the greater part of its foreign relations had to do with a very narrow range of episodic bilateralisms covering the Soviet Union, Eastern Europe and selective parts of the Third World.

Even as China entered the United Nations (UN), it still drew largely on its own domestic political experience in its adaptation to international alignments. To combat 'hegemonism', Chinese foreign policy encouraged the development of 'multipolarity', but the latter was conceptually understood on the basis of domestic historical understandings of political alignments during the pre-1949 revolutionary years of united front struggle. The latter was conceptualized at the international level in terms of Mao Zedong's theory of 'three worlds'.[1]

China had contemporaneously experienced multiple colonialisms and was self-professedly wary of 'power politics', but was looking for recognition of its own sovereign importance. If this importance had been denied for far too long, China was still reluctant to undertake great responsibilities in international affairs as it was a developing state with finite resources. Even now, the PRC plays a cautious role on the UN Security Council, often preferring abstaining rather than vetoing resolutions. Chinese diplomacy is beginning to see that China must bear new responsibilities, but it has often reiterated the continuing importance of state sovereignty. Its defense strategy was, and for the most part still is, conceptually subordinated to its own goals of national economic development.

As late as 1997, scholars like Samuel Kim claimed that the PRC did not even have an Asia-Pacific regional policy. Kim focused on the 'ambivalence' of PRC regionalism: 'Although most of the country's external relations pivot around the Asia-Pacific region, Peking seldom articulated any coherent definition of its place in Asian international relations.' In effect, Kim tried to put the PRC on the psychiatrist's couch. He believed that he had uncovered a fundamental paradox in the Chinese quest for identity as a new world power:

> The PRC's quest for an appropriate niche in a changing international order can be seen as an ongoing struggle to enhance physical and psychological well-being, in the course of which the Self attempts to secure an identity as global power that others do not bestow, while others attempt to bestow an identity as a regional power that the Self does not appropriate.[2]

Now, however, Chinese analysis is 'maturely' exploring the policy consequences of what was perhaps an anachronistic preoccupation with the injustices and humiliations of historical imperialism and Cold War containment. The PRC's entry into the World Trade Organization (WTO) was accompanied by domestic foreign policy debates on China as becoming a 'normal country' (*zhengchangole guojia*). The debate was filliped by Jiang Zemin's July 1, 2001 speech commemorating the 80th anniversary of the Chinese Communist Party. The speech was widely interpreted as a key gloss on the history of the struggles of the Chinese people as it relates to the contemporary need for China to put the history of national humiliation truly in the past so that China can properly achieve its rightful status as a new world power. In short, any tendency to historical melancholy hardly suits the image of China as a newly emerging responsible world power on the international stage.[3]

Perhaps even more interesting is the contemporary Chinese claim that China as a world power is more predisposed to accepting the responsibilities of citizenship in the international community than is the United States. Some sense of the change of rhetoric and policy can be gleaned from contemporary Chinese leadership comment to the effect that China has remained 'sober' even in the apparently ugly face of American 'perversity'. Responding to US unilateralism, Jiang Zemin claimed with great composure and equanimity: 'Even if the US is perverse, there is no reason why China should act as the US does.'[4]

The political and diplomatic implications of such sobriety are very interesting. Although Chinese revisionism seeks greater political equality in the affairs of states, as a world power that must deal responsibly with the inevitable contradictions underlying world politics, China is advocating the adroit adaptation to 'the dialectical relationship between competition and compromise'.

The following analysis from the Chinese Communist Party's Central Party School likens international relations to a mechanical metaphor of 'grinding and fitting':

> 'Grinding and fitting' is originally a mechanical and physical concept, but it is also applicable to international relations. ...Struggle certainly exists, but it does not necessarily lead to the elimination of one side by the other. In most cases, both sides finally conclude a compromise through bargaining back and forth in the course of grinding and fitting. There may be a win-win result, or maybe one side will gain something more. In

principle, the relations between most countries in the world are relations of competition. ...While handling foreign relations issues, our country may also encounter contradictions with other countries, and struggle may appear around these contradictions. However, our purpose should not be winning absolutely and defeating the other side completely. The struggle must be restrained from going too far. Only by keeping a sense of propriety in the handling of international relations issues can we act on just grounds, to our advantage, and with restraint, and properly combine our principles with flexibility.

Therefore, in the future international arena, we should adroitly master and apply the dialectical relationship between competition and compromise.[5]

Chinese 'sobriety' is analytically interesting in that it conflicts with the assumption of a 'China threat' and lends support to the building of international regimes through multilateralism. Chinese policy does reflect a realism that acknowledges that the balance of power is a real concern in today's world, but this realism is commingled with an idealism regarding mutual respect and the community of interests between equal sovereign states. The latter now figures largely in Chinese analytical assumptions concerning the potentially positive relationship between regionalism and globalization. Related Chinese policy principles are being carried across regional and international organization. The latter have been articulated in a context of significant Chinese participation in the new regional contexts of the Asia Pacific Economic Cooperation (APEC), the ASEAN-Post Ministerial Conference (ASEAN-PMC) and the ASEAN Regional Forum (ARF).

Chinese diplomacy has strenuously supported the 'APEC approach' and 'the Spirit of the Big Community' that respects national self-determination through a strategy of flexible adaptation to diversity, and gradual advancement based on equality and mutual respect, cooperation, and voluntary action.[6] The Chinese sensitivity towards different stages of development also informs Chinese advocacy of 'common prosperity' and 'shared development'.

Differences of culture in the state system, on the other hand, require the adoption of 'seeking common ground while reserving differences' (*qiutong cunyi*) as the basis for state-to-state relations. This formulation advocates reciprocity and equality in the peaceful dialogue between traditions and cultures and hence this principle is asserted against Samuel Huntington's thesis on the 'clash of civilizations'.

More recently, these ideas have been advocated in terms of a parallel notion of 'common security'. From the Chinese perspective the new Shanghai Cooperation Organization embodies this same value system in world affairs. The 2001 metamorphosis of the 'Shanghai Five' into the Shanghai Cooperation Organization (SCO) that includes the Republic of Kazakhstan, the PRC, the Kyrgyz Republic, the Russian Federation and the Republics of Tajikistan and Uzbekistan, has, for example, been highlighted as a progressive 'regrouping and cooperation mechanism' that supports the 'regionalization of Eurasia'. The latter in turn supports a beneficial multipolar process and the establishment of a new international political *and* economic order.[7]

In response to what it sometimes refers to as a 'new regionalism', Chinese policy principles still draw upon historical preferences emphasizing reciprocity between sovereign states. The June 15, 2001 Declaration of the Shanghai Cooperation Organization, for example, refers under its fourth principle to the SCO's 'Shanghai spirit'. The latter has its intellectual antecedents in the 'APEC approach'. The 'Shanghai Spirit' emphasizes the handling of state-to-state relations on the familiar basis of equality, consultation, mutual confidence, mutual benefit, respect, solidarity, and cooperation and converges with historical principles such as 'seek common ground and reserve differences' and the five principles of peaceful coexistence. It is on the basis of these updated Cold War principles that the Chinese are pursuing a more vigorous approach to multilateralism at both the international and regional level. At the same time this reconfigured emphasis on state sovereignty informs the Chinese adaptation to globalization.

In the late 1980s scholars began to debate the Chinese foreign policy perspective on economic interdependence and the extent to which China would be prepared to adapt to neo-liberalism. Taibei scholar, Chih-yu Shih, for example, correlated the PRC's 'search for independence in an interdependent world' within the antithesis of an apparently healthy neo-realist response to the realities of the global market and a historical political focus on foreign policy independence. The latter had apparently exaggerated the importance of state sovereignty and had 'blocked China's full participation in the world economy'.[8]

Even now Western scholars disagree on the nature and extent of contemporary Chinese concession to neo-liberalism. In fact, in this volume, Ann Kent makes a very different but interesting argument that the Chinese, rather than having 'blocked' themselves, have actually jumped over Rooseveltian 'internationalism' directly into contemporary 'globalization' with the result that their subscription to neo-liberalism has been rather unqualified and has worked at the expense of domestic social justice and related human rights.

One might argue, however, that if the Leninist thesis on imperialism as the highest stage of capitalism has been significantly revised, it still has significant contemporary implications. The exploitative relation between developing and developed economies is still a serious policy concern, but the final conflict between the socialist and capitalist systems is neither imminent, nor even relevant. There is a new rationality that regards economic globalization as inexorable, but also controllable. Foreign policy is no longer focused on the collapse of the capitalist system, but participation in economic globalization is qualified in ongoing recognition of the power politics of developed states that are manipulating the multilateral terms of trade and investment.

Chinese analysis has fewer and fewer stated qualms about extolling China's status as a 'big market power' and 'big human resource power'. Domestic ideology now more or less accepts the role of the labor market in the transition to the 'socialist' market and, at the international level, the cheapness of Chinese labor is hailed as a 'comparative advantage'.

Does this mean that Adam Smith has won, and Marx is condemned to irrelevance? In his assessment of 'economic globalization' and 'comparative advantage', Professor Chen Qingxiu defined 'economic globalization' as: 'the inevitable consequence of the development of productivity' and as 'a worldwide industrial adjustment process that is dominated by the developed countries' and 'mainly driven by multinational companies' that are thriving in an 'integrated world market'.[9] In order to deal with this 'inevitable' process, Chen advised that China turn its low labor costs into a comparative advantage. While he opined that no country can resist globalization as an 'irreversible trend', he warned the weak developing countries not to become overly dependent upon the transnational flow of capital.

Various authors have tracked the related definition of 'globalization', but the differences often seem less important than the similarities. He Liping of the China Institute of Finance and Banking, for example, stated:

> Globalization, put quite simply, may be seen as a process in which factors of production flow across borders in a fairly free way, resulting in rapid expansion in trade and investment flows. [The related impact results] in increases in hardware technology and consumer utility accompanied by trade and foreign investment flows; increases in employment opportunities; and increases in capital supply.[10]

Chinese policy and diplomacy does not hesitate to advise Third World developing countries that they must find ways to maximize the opportunities of economic globalization while retaining their sovereign options through participation in international rule-making and remaining politically wary of the agenda-setting activity of the developed states. Zhang Yijun of the Chinese Institute of Foreign Affairs has, for example, tendered the following free advice:

> ... it is imperative to pursue an open policy and deepen reform, strive to seek advantages while avoiding disadvantages in dealing with other countries and promote what is beneficial and abolish what is harmful domestically. While observing universally accepted international rules and making good use of all possibilities in these rules to create opportunities for their own development, it is essential to fight for greater voice in the formulation and modification of these rules at the same time, in order to make them more rational. Facts have shown that [this] is workable though the road is arduous.[11]

In his September 11, 1999 speech to APEC business leaders, Jiang Zemin once again drew attention to 'economic globalization' as a 'double-edged sword': 'Like a double-edged sword, it poses to all countries, the developing countries in particular, the new problem of how to safeguard their economic security while accelerating market opening, intensifying competition and improving efficiency.'[12]

Lu Yafan wrote that the benefits of such globalization will not accrue at the same rate in all countries and regions and that 'spontaneous market behavior' is more likely to benefit the developed states and that free trade can easily encroach on the economic sovereignty of 'developing countries'. Having said this, Lu still came to the conclusion that developing countries can survive only through 'active participation'. He suggested: 'Developing countries cannot stay outside globalization only because of the risks and negative factors. If they move in contradiction to the trend, they will only lag more behind...' [13]

Chinese analysis acknowledges the possibility of economic globalization turning into 'global Americanization';[14] however, such analysis often suggests that, if there is an unevenness in the distribution of interdependence, significant variation in states' 'vulnerabilities' and 'sensibilities' and a disproportionate reliance of the developing countries on the developed countries, even the developed, let alone the developing countries will seek to modify the consequences of transnational interdependence.[15]

The unevenness in the process of economic globalization did not, however, distract China's former Party chief, Jiang Zemin, from endorsing a twin policy of 'bringing in' and 'going out'. 'Bringing in' required policy expediency with regard to the expansion of foreign investment in the PRC, but with China's entry into the WTO there was new contemporaneous policy emphasis on 'going out' as, for example, explained by Chen Jian, Deputy Minister, Foreign Trade and Economic Cooperation:

> ... to accelerate implementing the 'going out' strategy is urgently needed for participating in economic globalization and [to] expand the space for economic development; it is needed for deepening our country's relations with the developing countries in order to attain joint development; for exercising China's rights in the WTO and raising the level of opening up; for spurring a strategic restructuring of China's economy; for safeguarding China's economic security and realizing a sustainable development of the national economy; and for bringing into shape [a] Chinese type of transnational corporation and increasing China's competitiveness in the international community.[16]

Also, Chinese analysis is now recommending to the developing countries that they might even learn from the history of market capitalism in the developed states of Western Europe and North America. The 1999 China Human Development report for the UNDP, 'Transition and the State', claimed that the introduction of markets in the developed countries often required state intervention.

Apparently, in those parts of the world where market institutions are well established they did not simply emerge spontaneously, but rather often depended heavily on state actions and hence the role of laissez-faire economics has been greatly exaggerated:

> ... The study of the rise of the market economy in England finds that the road to the free market was opened and kept open by an enormous increase

in continuous, centrally organized and controlled interventionism. Such interventionism, was, if anything greater in the countries that underwent industrialization after England did. As the cases of the United States, Japan and East Asian NIEs [Newly Industrialized Economies] illustrate, the historical route to human development has not been via laissez-faire regimes.[17]

While calls to bring down the capitalist system have been replaced by calls for export-led economic growth, Chinese analysis still continues to profess deliberately a 'dialectical', if not an ideological, understanding of the relation between 'economic globalization' and state sovereignty as a 'unity of opposites'. Such dialectics encompass contradictions and opportunities, gains and losses and prospective cooperation and competition. Great change in the international situation has required more 'opening', but policy still presumes that globalization can be managed to support national economic development on an ideal basis of 'peace and development'.

Apparently, Deng Xiaoping's theoretical genius further developed Marx's idea of world history. At any rate, his theory has often been co-opted to legitimate Chinese attempts to protect Chinese sovereignty and at the same time to secure an improved standard of living through participation in investment and in the technological opportunities of economic globalization.[18]

As authors like Ann Kent and Margaret Pearson point out in this volume, the PRC is, itself, on a steep learning curve as it deals with the rapidly mutating and palpable contradictions of 'globalization'. While reiterating the importance of state sovereignty within its 'independent foreign policy', China has recently entered into the WTO as a new inductee. This entry came at the height of renewed debate about China's participation in 'globalization'.

The issue of 'openness' as it connects with globalization reflects the changing policy perspective on state sovereignty and free trade. Whereas there was in the past a preference merely for 'economic cooperation' between sovereign states there is now a new enthusiasm for the building of free trade zones. This is to move beyond early APEC ideas on 'free trade in the area' as distinct from 'free trade areas', per se. The former only required 'open regionalism' and the voluntary reduction of tariffs on an ad hoc basis with any trading partner. In the early days of APEC this meant a more flexible viewpoint on the question of state sovereignty even as the latter's importance was reiterated.

There is now much Chinese analytical commentary as to how regional free trade supports multilateralism and economic globalization. The influential newspaper, the *Da Kung Pao*, in Hong Kong, for example, quoted one of the PRC's most senior economists, Ma Hong, and hailed China's prospective participation in the China-ASEAN free-trade region as an important step in a new process of regional economic cooperation; and it was argued: '... the pattern of setting up a free-trade region is a favorable direction for China to develop the relationship of regional grouping and regional alliance (*jituanhua he guyu lianmeng guanxi*).[19]

Moreover adaptation to economic globalization required China's participation in a new international politics supporting a wider-based and revisionist conception of the 'rules of the game' in international trade and investment. The Beijing *Liaowang* newspaper, for example, suggested that the developing countries might learn to participate in the making of such rules:

> Economic globalization is a 'double-edged sword' ...it can, through cross-border capital flows, technological exchanges, and reasonable deployment of major means of production, deepen interdependence and promote economic development of various countries in the world, and provide development opportunities for various countries, seizing the initiative of writing the international economic 'rules of the game'... [20]

While one could argue that the PRC was seriously disadvantaged in certain areas of negotiation such as anti-dumping, the WTO entry was billed as a new stage of China's 'opening' to the world. Entry was internally legitimized as an opportunity for further domestic economic development, but it has not finally resolved the domestic issue of sovereignty.

One key motive for entry was in fact sovereign equality itself, as explained, for example, in the following pro-regime *Wen Wei Po* editorial opinion:

> China's 'WTO entry' also signifies that China no longer has to stand on the sidelines while other countries draw up regulations to which it has to adapt. On the contrary, it can totally participate in and draw up rules of competition for the new century in negotiations through a multilateral trading system and become the beneficiary of certain relevant regulations to ensure China's equal entry into the world market.[21]

China's serious adaptation to multilateralism is evident in the fact that under Washington's pressure, the PRC's negotiators made major concessions, and not just compromises in order to get a seat at the WTO table. In effect China's progressive 'open door' approach to 'economic globalization' remains rooted in domestic policy designed to support China's domestic economic development. The latter requires that China not be marginalized in multilateral fora that determine the rules of play, and it requires that the PRC, in its own national interest, campaign with alacrity against the new dangers of protectionism. What is new in this is the positive calculation that China can, through hopefully adroit participation in mulilateralism, seize the benefits of cooperation while minimizing the harmful dimensions of foreign economic dominance of the international trading system.

Multilateralism has become the extravagantly advertised new instrument for the achievement of domestic economic goals. The WTO is compared to an 'economic United Nations' where state sovereignty deals with the rules of the international trading game. While status quo powers might have at least implicit misgivings about Chinese revisionist support of multipolarity, the new Chinese focus on the importance of involvement in multilateral rule-making might be welcomed as a positive element in China's adaptation to its responsibilities as a new world power.

This adaptation to multilateralism has also been taking place in other spheres relating, for example, to security and human rights. Even in the immediate context of Western censure and trade sanctions after Tiananmen Square, the PRC, in what seems to have been a counterintuitive move, formally accepted the legitimacy and domestic applicability of 'human rights' terminology. Although formal statements of intent have not satisfied China's critics and the Chinese, themselves, have noted real problems relating to 'authenticity' (or the actual enjoyment of legislated human rights), a new wave of accession to international treaties has followed, as has a new generation of human rights law and regulation relating, for example, to the rights and interests of women, children, labor, the handicapped and the elderly. There has been related non-governmental organization (NGO)-formation inside China;[22] and there has since been an annual, albeit acrimonious, exchange with the State Department over its specific reporting on China's human rights performance.

In the security sphere, there is adaptation to changing technology as well as changing international regimes and political structures. The Revolution in Military Technology has called for progressive demobilization of conventional forces and changes in strategic thinking about the nature and scope of threat and war.[23] In the face of technological advancement, the people's war has become a distant memory. Chinese diplomacy, however, has continuously stressed 'independent foreign policy' and 'seeking common ground while reserving differences', good neighborliness and 'the five principles of peaceful coexistence'.

China's military diplomacy and its 'new security concept' are based upon a new application of apparently established principles in a new world confronted by the changing requirements of globalization. When it comes to the economic relations between states, Chinese policy has stressed the opportunities for 'common prosperity' and 'common development'. The same underlying themes relating to reciprocity and mutuality between states that are equally sovereign is stressed in security terms. In particular the US quest for 'absolute security' is contrasted with the need for a security community, based upon sovereign equality. The Chinese are attempting to blunt the potentially destabilizing aspects of the Revolution in Military Affairs, particularly as the power relations between states are affected by unevenness in the military technological capacity of states to participate in high-tech weapons development.

On the one hand, contemporary Chinese foreign policy claims a progressive continuity with past notions to the effect that China, as a developing state that experienced the full force of imperialism, will not compromise the security of other states through participation in great power alliances and the strategic placement of military forces on foreign soil.

On the other hand, the 'new' part of their 'new security concept relates to the post-Cold War need to focus on 'comprehensive security'. The latter is no longer defined in the exclusively unidimensional, balance-of-power terms of military force. The new concept adapts to the consequences of economic globalization as the economic dimensions of security are deliberately correlated with the changing social, cultural and political aspects of world politics.

The new concept asserts collective security, as it is supported in 'common development', and, as it resists the inequities of balance-of-power realism. These correlations are then used to legitimate China's wider participation in international and regional multilateral security fora. The 1998 white paper on defense, for example, endorsed a notion of security community versus the allegedly unfair and unstable features of Cold War military alliances that threatened the sovereignty of the developing states:

> History has proved that the concepts and systems of security with military alliances as the basis and increasing military might as the means could not be conducive to peace during the Cold War. Under the new situation, especially, enlarging military blocs and strengthening military alliances run counter to the tide of the times. Security cannot be guaranteed by an increase in arms, nor by military alliances. Security should be based on mutual trust and common interests. We should promote trust through dialogue, seek security through cooperation, respect each other's sovereignty, solve disputes through peaceful means and strive for common development. To obtain lasting peace it is imperative to abandon the Cold war mentality, cultivate a new concept of security and seek a new way to safeguard peace.[24]

Dialectics still underlie the new Chinese attitude not only towards economic globalization, but also towards cultural globalization. Cultures are distinct and yet they interpenetrate one another. And this has also raised issues of legitimate localization of international human rights standards versus cultural relativism. The 'clash of civilization' is vociferously challenged in Chinese analysis that updates the Cold War principle of 'seeking common ground, while reserving differences' to deal with the stresses and strains that characterize the relations between different states and cultures.

The disposition and strength of cultural diversity is also tied to economic globalization. To insure sufficient space for such diversity vis-à-vis 'global Americanization', the Chinese analysis also emphasizes both multipolarity and the ever-widening circles of consensus within multilateralism. Chinese policy thinking stresses that economic globalization can generate opportunities among the developing countries so as to contest the singular position of the American economy.

Moreover, this thinking emphasizes the possibility of economic globalization as a new and more intense cycle of competition as states move from industrial modernization into the era of high-tech and informational revolution. Related competition between the big powers may well create 'new diversified power space' and a 'power shift' away from the status quo of American domination. In sum, states' adaptation to economic globalization rather than favoring inexorable capital formation in favor of the single superpower will create new opportunities for multipolarization as the influence of various countries rise and fall.[25]

All of the above suggests that Chinese policy still reflects the revisionist concerns of a developing state that has been through a specific historical experience with imperialism and yet this policy has increasingly come to terms with the more recent complexities of globalization. The following articles provide several key perspectives on China's adaptation as a revisionist world power to the opportunities and challenges of globalization. When taken together these contributions offer the reader a ledger of pluses and minuses in terms of the PRC's conceptual and practical attempt as a new world power to manage the rapidly developing contradictions of globalization.

Ann Kent, in her article, for example, reviews the changing dimensions of 'internationalization' and 'globalization' to emphasize the rather forced character of China's telescoped response to neo-liberalism in the current stage of 'globalization'. The PRC in effect leapfrogged over 'Rooseveltian internationalism' which originally included a kinder focus on social justice, and this has apparently adversely affected the Chinese commitment to human rights in the contemporary context of an unqualified and accelerated adaptation to new market relationships and competitive mechanisms. In this scenario, the Chinese have not had sufficient international experience and composure to resist the blandishments of a triumphal neo-liberalism.

Quite literally, the Chinese are unable to get off the 'treadmill of growth'. In seizing the opportunities of economic globalization so as to sustain high rates of annual growth the Chinese leadership has been caught up in a human rights trade-off that imperils the 'physical and social wellbeing of its citizens'. Ann Kent examines these related assumptions with specific reference to China's participation in the World Trade Organization and to China's interactions with the World Health Organization and the initial PRC failure to respond to the SARS virus. She agrees with Pitman Potter's assessment that 'the effect of China's WTO-driven legal reforms has been to privilege market actors, the goals of social stability and central government control, rather than offering human rights protection' (p. 531). And secondly with respect to the Chinese government's handling of SARS, the weakness of Chinese participation in international organization is traced to flaws in local political culture and administration.

In their article, Professors Alan Smart and Jinn-Yu Hsu explore yet another dimension of 'globalization'. They recognize that the term, 'globalization' is, itself, 'intensely contested', but they argue that at its core, it conveys 'the creation of a global capitalist economy, the stitching together of production processes in multiple nations (the "global factory") and the heightened maintenance of transnational ties by migrants and other citizens' (p. 545). Especially in light of the arbitrary ambiguities of China's 'socialist market' and underdeveloped legal system, they are impressed with the robust flexibility in overseas Chinese investor participation in China's economy.

The highly successful transition to the market and the openness to foreign investment has occurred without basic regime change in a context of legally uncertain property rights. In fact, it might be argued that political connections have meant more in this uncertain business environment than recent 'rule of law' developments inside the PRC. In particular, Smart and Hsu explore specifically how overseas Chinese FDI facilitated the first stages of China's 'open door' and then they turn to an interesting comparative analysis of how overseas Chinese technical and business frameworks are now flexible strategies for participating in Chinese high technology development.

But can the PRC, as a developing state, really claim the status of a new world power, or is the PRC the likely victim of a controlling globalization process, largely led by the US, that will ultimately hobble Chinese sovereignty? Many observers have treated China's induction into the WTO as a major breakthrough in terms of China's convergence with the norms and requirements of the world economy. Margaret Pearson in her article focuses attention on yet another piece of the globalization puzzle when she inquires as to the implications of China's WTO accession in terms of fit between China's trade and regulatory policies and the WTO's globalized norms and requirements.

As was earlier mentioned, the Chinese see in economic globalization not only power shifts but diversified space wherein it becomes possible for different sovereign countries to not only cope with, but creatively to seek the advantage of new investment and technological opportunities without having to compromise irrevocably their own state structures and control over their own economies. Also, while this is undoubtedly a matter of controversy, the Chinese are not above pointing out that even the US has historically used the state to intervene in the building of the national economy.

While anticipating that the WTO accession will have a deep impact on domestic economic, administrative and judicial systems, Professor Pearson emphasizes that regardless of the disposition of state ownership and management of enterprise, China, like other WTO members, still has an enormous capacity for state regulation within its own potentially mixed model of state regulation. The Chinese may well respond to the continuing domestic political discourse on economic nationalism through a selective adaptation to elements from both the Anglo-American and developmental models of economic regulation. Pearson draws a conclusion that is in some rough sense parallel to the above Chinese argument, but she draws it independently from the comparative and international political economy literature. The latter argues that countries within the WTO need not all converge to the same expected narrow norm of regulatory structures that is widely anticipated in US business circles.

Even as the WTO moves inside China's borders to deal with impediments to trade, the Chinese sovereign ability to manage their own economy will not necessarily be irreversibly compromised, as the WTO, itself, accepts '"wide bands" of acceptable rules, institutional arrangements, and behavior', and as states have still significant discretion as to how they might ingeniously apply domestic regulation so as to conform with WTO requirements and norms. In the final analysis, Pearson does not require China's unqualified convergence with the Anglo-American model of economic regulation.

The above analysis suggests that despite the burden of history the Chinese response to globalization has become quite sophisticated. They are becoming self-consciously adept at wielding learning the 'double-edged sword'. State sovereignty and economic globalization have not been placed in exclusive opposition, but instead Chinese policy dialectics have explored both the positive and negative possibilities of state adaptation to the opportunities of economic globalization.

This is not to say that the internal lines of policy have not changed substantively over the years since Deng Xiaoping first set out the 'open door policy' in 1979. Prior to Deng, foreign aid was unacceptable and direct foreign investment was negligible. When the 'open door' was first introduced it came with qualifications regarding the assurance of China's 'self-reliance'. For a long time free trade was seen as a threatening neo-liberal sword that extended to the very heart of the Chinese socialist state.

In his accompanying article, Dr. Kevin Cai delves into the proliferating literature of PRC scholarly think-tanks and research institutes. He shows just how far Chinese policy thinking and perspective has advanced with reference to the recent decision to form a Free Trade Association with ASEAN, as well as with reference to the new attitude on the staged creation of an East Asian Free Trade Area. Cai explores the underlying controversies and reasonings that have resulted in a sea change in Chinese thinking regarding participation in free trade areas as the means of supporting China's goals for national economic development.

Chinese analysis is self-consciously focusing on a new regionalism. There is a range of Chinese policy opinion, but to a certain extent the latter picks up on the original 1993 Seattle notion at the inception of APEC, namely, that the fostering of Asia Pacific regional fora such as APEC would expedite the final negotiations of the Uruguay Round and the subsequent extension of Most Favored Nation status (MFN). On the basis of Asian principles of flexibility, consensus and voluntariness, Chinese policy supported APEC's 'open regionalism' that highlighted tariff reduction, based on the voluntary extension of regional and extra-regional MFN, as against protective bloc regionalism. In the early to mid-1990s, there was some reluctance to consider a rule-bound free trade area that might have unpredictable implications for China's economy and state sovereignty.[26] Within the councils and working groups of APEC, the Chinese position substantively supported the balancing of trade and investment liberalization with development through economic and technical cooperation and operationally it endorsed 'the principle of independent decision-making and voluntary participation' (*zizhu zhiyuan yuanze*).[27]

According to Kevin Cai's analysis, a more radical change in perspective occurred with the 1997 Asian financial crisis. The latter highlighted the increasing economic integration among China, Japan, South Korea, Taiwan and Hong Kong, and Chinese policy perspective exhibited an increasing sensitivity to the spread of free trade areas elsewhere in the world. Moreover, the Free Trade Agreement (FTA) was progressively perceived as involving fewer and less serious political costs. After all, it was but a lower form of integration. Furthermore Chinese perspective increasingly emphasized the need to participate in regional economic organization so as to influence the 'rules of the game' as these are developed within international multilateral fora and institutions. From within the newly emerging regional context the Chinese prepared to take a more active leadership role to help foster a step by step approach to the FTA in East Asia.

One of the most recent examples of a more confident and sophisticated Chinese leadership approach to regionalism is explored in the article by Sun Zhuangzhi, Director of the Central Asian Department of the Institute for East European, Russian and Central Asian Studies, at the Chinese Academy of Social Sciences. Sun's contribution provides a good example of the new thinking about the interaction of old and new regionalism in the post-9/11 world. His analysis reviews significant historical continuities in the balance-of-power politics of Central Asia while at the same time it considers globalization and the new linkage between regional and international multilateralism.

On June 14 and 15, 2001, the original 'Shanghai Five', including the PRC, Russia, Kazakhstan, Kyrgyzstan, and Tajikistan joined with Uzbekistan to form the new Shanghai Cooperation Organization. This 'Organization' is only just getting off the ground, but it reflects the extension of APEC principles relating to the flexible adaptation to different stages of development and national economic objectives, as well as to the new notion of 'comprehensive security' as it brings together considerations of economic and security cooperation. Moreover, regional and international security concerns are deliberately entwined in the fashioning of new regional policy perspective.

This new organization has not only to deal with extremism and separatism, in effect, the continuing ramifications of the distintegration of the Soviet Union and its reverberating impact on the fragile integrity of the new Central Asian republics, but also with the rapidly expanding frontiers of post-9/11 international terrorism, religious extremism and the disintegrative tendencies of sectarian nationalism. While the difficulties of regional confidence building are not underestimated, the aforementioned 'Shanghai Spirit' has highlighted regional multilateralism based largely on the non-aligned need for a security community and for 'common development' among economies that are very uneven in their development.

Not only is the term, 'globalization', hotly contested, but the various processes that are often associated with the term represent an extraordinary gamut of political, social, economic and cultural experience. The authors in this volume have, however, brought together a number of interesting perspectives on the main issue as to how China will cope as a new world power in dealing with the plethora of contradictions inherent in these processes.

CONCLUSION

The various authors in this volume have suggested, the PRC faces serious practical problems in adapting to the challenges and opportunities of globalization as a new world power, and as a developing state that is straining to deal with increasingly significant issues of social justice and human rights. However, despite the burden of history and the late start in 'opening' to the rest of the world, Chinese policy has achieved a new level of sophistication. Free trade is no longer automatically antithetical to state sovereignty, and China is taking the lead in helping to craft a new regionalism. Chinese foreign policy and military diplomacy are sponsoring 'new regionalism', 'common development' and a new security concept based on 'community' as opposed to the 'balance of power'.

At least at a conceptual level, it seems as though Chinese foreign policy dialectics are adequate to the understanding of the rapidly mutating contradictions of globalization. Such complex policy rejects any foreign labeling as 'neo-realist', but it self-consciously incorporates a revisionist pragmatism. It is no longer concerned with the collapse of capitalism; it accepts globalization as inevitable, but the latter's opportunities can be maximized, and its liabilities, managed. Such policy is still revisionist in its assertion of the principles of sovereign state equality and mutual development versus great power attempts to achieve dominance and 'absolute security'. It is also seemingly idealist in its preference for collective security and multilateralism. However, Chinese confidence in the latter is entwined with a cautionary sense of power alignment that sees multilateralism in strategic synthesis with multipolarity.

While pursuing the opportunities of economic globalization and lobbying for more favorable 'rules of the game', the Chinese revisionist approach to multilateralism still considers economic globalization as a 'double-edged sword'. Based upon experience as a developing state, the PRC, as a relatively new and emerging world power, has attempted to appropriate the original Westphalian principles of national self-determination and sovereign state equality in a mixed idealist/realist challenge to the hierarchical features of 'neo-liberal' globalization.

The PRC now has not only an Asia-Pacific regional strategy, but it has a new leadership approach to multilateralism that entwines its principles and experience at the Asia-Pacific regional level with increasingly well-defined international perspective and policy priorities. Chinese foreign policy thinking is coherently focused. Most importantly, there is a responsible new flexibility in the Chinese view of state sovereignty in the new era of globalization.

NOTES

The author would like to thank the Social Sciences and Humanities Research Council of Canada for related funding.

1. See King C. Chen (ed.), *China and the Three Worlds* (White Plains, New York: M.E. Sharpe, 1979), *passim*; and also R.C. Keith, 'The Origins and Strategic Implications of China's "Independent Foreign Policy"', *International Journal*, Vol. xli, No. 1 (Winter 1985–86), pp. 115–17.
2. Samuel S. Kim, 'Mainland China in a Changing Asia-Pacific Regional Order', *Issues and Studies*, Vol. 30, No. 10 (Oct. 1994), p. 5.
3. Pang Zhongying, 'People's Observations: China's International Status and Foreign Strategy after the Cold War', *Renmin wang* (People's outlook) May 5, 2002, FBIS-CHI-2002–0506, pp. 8–9, 13.
4. Jiang Zemin's May 9, 2001 speech to the Hong Kong Fortune Global Forum as cited in R.C. Keith, 'Strategic Ambiguity and the New Bush Administration's "China Threat"', *The Review of*

International Affairs, Vol. 1, No. 2 (Winter 2001), p. 17. For an interesting critique of US failure to honor its own values of equality and mutual respect in international relations, see Wang Yusheng, 'Is this the Term of "Mutual Respect" Defined in the American Dictionary', *Waijiao jikan* (Foreign Affairs Journal), No. 64 (June 2002), pp. 68–71.

5. Li Zhongjie, 'Our Country Needs an International Strategy at a Higher Level – Past Erght on How to Understand and Approach the Current International Strategic Situation', *Liaowang*, Aug. 2, 2002, in PBIS-CHI-2002-0813, online at http://80-wnc.fedworld.gov.ezproxy.lib ... gleo3dde8w&CID=C85263061523437523770371.

6. See, for example, Wang Yusheng's explanations in 'APEC, ASEM, SCO and New Security Outlook', *Foreign Affairs Journal*, No. 64 (June 2002), p. 72.

7. Xia Yishan, 'The Shanghai Cooperation Organization As I See [It]', *Foreign Affairs Journal*, No. 61 (Sept. 2001), p. 11.

8. Chih-yu Shih, *Interdependence, Independence and Chinese Neorealism*, Working Paper No. 59 (Toronto: Joint Center for Asia-Pacific Studies, 1993), pp. 6–7.

9. Chen Qingxiu, 'Jingji quanqiuhua yu biljiao youshi', (Economic globalization and comparative advantage), *Guangdong xingzhengxueyuan xuebao* (*Journal of Guangdong Institute of Public Administration*), Vol 14, No. 4, Aug. 2002, p. 63.

10. He Liping, 'The Impact of Globalization on China: An Assessment with Regard to China's Reforms and Liberalization', *World Economy and China*, No. 6 (2000), p. 7.

11. Zhang Yijun, 'Globalization, Multi-Polarity, Uni-Polarity and Americanization', *Foreign Affairs Journal*, 2001, copied from *World Economy and Politics*, No. 12 (2000), p. 18.

12. As quoted by Zhang Yijun, 'Economic Globalization and State Sovereignty', *Foreign Affairs Journal*, No. 58 (Dec. 2000), p. 16.

13. Lu Yafan, '21 Shiji Woguo fuhe miandui jingji quanqiuhuade sikao' (Thoughts on how China should face economic globalization in the twenty-first century), *Dongbei shifan daxue xuebao* (Northeastern teacher's college bulletin), No. 2 (2000), pp. 45–6.

14. Ibid., p. 18.

15. Lu Changhiu, 'Jingji quanqiuhua yu shijie xingshi' (Economic globalization and world conditions), *Guoji wenti yanjiu* (International studies), No. 2 (2002), pp. 26–7.

16. Gong Wen, '" Bringing in" and "Going Out" Are Two Approaches to Promote Opening Up', *Renmin ribao* (People's daily), FBIS, Daily Report, Dec. 7, 2002.

17. Zhang Yijun, 'Economic Globalization and State Sovereignty', p. 19.

18. For a related CCP defence of Deng's theories and policies, see Song Shichang and Li Ronghai, 'Globalization and the Formation of Socialism with Chinese Characteristics', in *Zhongguo shehui kexue* (Chinese social science), No. 3 (2002), pp. 106–11.

19. Ma Hong, 'China's Regional Economic relations in Asia Following its Accession to the WTO', *Ta Kung Pao*, April 20, 2002.

20. 'PRC's Liaowang Views Trend of Economic Globalization', Beijing *Liaowang*, No. 40, Oct. 1, 2001, p. 40, FBIS-CHI 2001-1011, available at: http://wnc.fedworld.gov/cgibin/retriev...s201b6377&CID=C211791992187500218628891. The *Renmin ribao* editorialized in almost the same way about the 'double-edged sword'. See, '*Renmin ribao* reviews WTO process, pros, cons of membership', RMRB, 11 Nov. 2001, p. 2, in FBIS-CHI*_2001–1112, p. 11, available at http://wnc.fedworld.gov/cgibin/retriev...7d01fvvwm&CID=C211791992187 500218628891.

21. 'WWP Editorial on Significance of Integrating PRC Economy with World through WTO', *Wen Wei Po*, 11 Nov. 2001, p. 4, available at: http;://wnc.fedworld.gov/egibin/retriev...zy01y23au&-CID=C211791992187500218628891.

22. See, for example, Ronald C. Keith, Zhiqiu Lin and Huang Lie, 'The Making of a Chinese NGO: A Case Study of the Research and Intervention Project on Domestic Violence', *Problems of Post Communism*, Vol. 50, No. 6 (Nov./Dec. 2003).

23. For discussion of the 'new security concept', see Ronald C. Keith, *The Chinese 'New Security Concept': The Revolution in Military Affairs, Space Weaponization and Prospective Arms Control Cooperation*, International Security Research and Outreach Programme, Department of Foreign Affairs, Canada, Dec. 2002, *passim*.

24. Ibid., p. 5.

25. Yu Zhengliang, 'Jingji quanqiuhua jinchengde xinshiji shijie geju' (The new world economic structure in the midst of economic globalization), *Fudan xuebao* (The Fudan university bulletin), No. 1, 2000, pp. 1–2.

26. Ronald C. Keith, 'Reflections on Sino-Canadian Cooperation in APEC', *Canadian Foreign Policy*, Vol. 5, No. 2 (Winter 1998), pp. 189–90.

27. Ibid., pp. 194–5.

China's Growth Treadmill: Globalization, Human Rights and International Relations

ANN KENT

China's rise as a world power, its remarkable economic and military development and its increasing international and regional influence owe much to globalization. On the surface, the country has integrated well into the new, interdependent world. However, from time to time the international community has been surprised by signs that all is not going as smoothly as China's flourishing market economy had led them to believe. For China, too, the process of integration has often had unintended consequences, not only for its domestic developments, in particular its human rights, but also for its international relations.

This article seeks to examine these unintended effects of globalization. In particular, it analyses the impact of China's entry into the international community at a time when the market ruled supreme in almost all fields of

Ann Kent is an Australian Research Fellow of the Australian Research Council at the Centre for International and Public Law, Faculty of Law, Australian National University.

endeavor. As against the view of some that China's problems stem from modernization policies that are too gradualist and still incomplete, it argues that the liberalization of China's economy has not been gradual enough. That China has embraced the market eagerly and swiftly without considering its impact on its citizens' human rights is perhaps not surprising in the light of its authoritarian political system. But it has also embraced the market without internalizing the sine qua non of market success – acceptance of the rule of law and the need for transparency in its international policies. The consequences of its selective acceptance of the norms of globalization and its partial integration into the international system are illustrated in an analysis of the impact of its entry into the World Trade Organization (WTO) and the World Health Organization (WHO) on its human rights and its international relations.

THE IMPACT OF HISTORY

The peculiar historical circumstances of China's entry into the international community have not received sufficient attention from Western scholars as an explanation for its international behavior and its domestic policies, although Chinese scholars consider them important.[1] The latter half of the nineteenth century, the twentieth and the early twenty-first centuries may be broadly divided into two interrelated but separate epochs: internationalization and globalization. While China, as Imperial China and Republican China, was integrated into the early phases of internationalization in the nineteenth and early twentieth centuries, the People's Republic of China (PRC) was largely excluded from the post-World War II phase of internationalization and only became a fully active participant in the international system and, more particularly, the international human rights system, from the 1980s, the period in which internationalization began to mutate into globalization. The PRC's absence from the international system in the critical years from 1949 to 1971, and, in particular, its exclusion from the United Nations, meant that it was largely deprived of the socializing influences of the distinct system of international values associated with that period.[2] Conversely, its full participation in the international system from the commencement of the globalization era made it susceptible to the norms dominating the new period, with neither knowledge nor experience of the offsetting constraints imposed by the prior international value systems.

Internationalization developed in three interrelated phases: (1) a predominantly functionalist internationalism in the late nineteenth and early twentieth centuries; (2) Wilsonian internationalism in the post-World War I period; and (3) Rooseveltian internationalism, from World War II. The first phase institutionalized the norm of interdependence in primary functional areas. In the third quarter of the nineteenth century, international conferences were convened pursuant to conflict and, in the final quarter, as a means of preventing conflict. These conferences, including the 1899 and 1907 Hague Conferences, also negotiated the early laws of war. Finally, the functionalist phase developed the concept of having a group of experts and administrators performing particular functions on behalf of a group of states.[3] From the 1870s to 1909, the number of intergovernmental organizations rose from 7 to 37, and that of international non-governmental organizations reached 176.[4] China, as Imperial China, joined its first international organization, the Universal Postal Union, in 1897, and sent delegations to the Hague Conferences.[5]

Wilsonian internationalism was largely a reaction to the horrors of World War I. The Paris Peace Conference of 1919, presided over by President Wilson, had undertaken the dual responsibility of making a peace settlement and fashioning an international system to ensure that such a devastating conflict could never be repeated. To promote international cooperation, peace and security it had to address not only collective security matters and the relations between states but pressing economic and social questions which had been highlighted by the growth of the trade union and socialist movements in the previous half century. The Covenant of the League of Nations, based on Wilson's vision, underwrote the establishment of the League of Nations, the Permanent Court of International Justice, itself originally inspired by the Hague Conferences, and the International Labour Organization. Although the Republic of China was integrated into this early international system through its participation at the Paris Peace Conference and its membership of the League, the latter's inability to constrain Japanese aggression in Manchuria undermined the mutual trust between China and the international community.

Rooseveltian internationalism, which built on the strengths of Wilsonian idealism and on the earlier functionalist tradition, represented a more complex and complete response to the violence and economic depredations of war, in this case World War II. Its norms were also institutionalized in a more rigorous way. Apart from its goals of collective security and the liberalization of international trade in an equitable manner, its foundations were strengthened by its amalgamation of US domestic norms of social justice, derived from the New Deal, with those of European welfare states. The robust international institutions to which it gave rise, namely the United Nations (UN) and the Bretton Woods institutions of international development, finance and trade – the World Bank, the International Monetary Fund, and the projected International Trade Organization – provided a holistic system of international norms incorporating individual and collective values of democracy, civil rights and social justice. This balance was reflected in the provisions of the UN Charter, which established in workable equilibrium the requirements of sovereignty, peace and security and individual human rights. It was also formalized in the 1948 Universal Declaration of Human Rights, which integrated civil, political, social, economic and cultural rights, in both individual and collective forms, and was implemented as binding international legal instruments in the International Covenant on Civil and Political Rights and the International Covenant on Economic, Social and Cultural Rights. The major achievements of this Rooseveltian era occurred in the 1940s. With the beginning of the Cold War, the social justice component of Roosevelt's initial conception was whittled away, and the norms of civil and political rights assumed ascendancy. In such an environment, the social justice aspects of the proposed International Trade

Organization, a formal international institution based on the vision of John Maynard Keynes, were sidelined, and one part of it, the General Agreement on Tariffs and Trade (GATT), which was initially simply a temporary multilateral agreement to provide a framework of rules and a forum to negotiate trade barrier reductions, became the principal forum of international trade regulation.[6]

The then Republic of China was one of the four great powers emerging from World War II which assisted in the negotiation and foundation of the UN. However, three years after the UN was established, the government of China changed, and the experience of the international system garnered by the Republic was transferred, along with the Nationalist government, to Taiwan. As a newly established socialist state, the People's Republic sought early on to replace Taiwan as the representative of 'China' in the United Nations. However, for a number of reasons, including US opposition to a communist state and the onset of the Korean War in 1950 which only heightened that opposition, it was unsuccessful. Its fate contrasted with that of the Soviet Union and Eastern European states, which not only benefited from UN membership but also from membership in regional organizations. The 'New China' shared with Rooseveltian internationalism a belief in social justice but, like the Soviet Union and Eastern European states, was also distinguished by its lack of respect for civil and political rights. The imbalance of rights flowing from its ideology was further entrenched by its treatment at the hands of the international community. Exclusion from the United Nations and from regional organizations denied it contact with an internationalist phase which otherwise might have acquainted it better with the norms of civil and political rights.[7] Only the Republic of China profited from such influences.

The PRC was also untouched by other international pressures which, over time, helped open up the socialist systems in the Soviet Union and Eastern European states. Even after 1971, when it finally replaced Taiwan as the representative of China in the United Nations, it did not become a target of international pressures to liberalize its human rights conditions because of its strategic usefulness to the West as a counterbalance to Soviet power. Again, unlike the Soviet Union and Eastern Europe, China was not a party to the Helsinki Accords of 1974, whereby Western recognition of the post-War territorial settlement of Eastern Europe became a quid pro quo for acceptance by the East of the need to expand their civil and political rights. As an opponent of Soviet 'social imperialism' in the 1970s, moreover, China was suspicious of the new ideas issuing from the Soviet Union, beginning with perestroika, the reform of the economic and political system, and developing, particularly after the disasters wrought by Chernobyl, into glasnost, which involved more openly consultative government and the wider dissemination of information. Taking a highly selective approach, China adopted only the economic form of perestroika, choosing to introduce a market system 'with Chinese characteristics', but maintaining its Leninist authoritarian political system and remaining closed to new political ideas and to the international goals of more open and transparent communication with the outside world.

As the PRC's involvement in international organizations increased, from its assumption of the China seat in the UN in 1971 to its full participation in international financial, developmental, security and human rights organizations in the 1980s, its approach to globalization was equally selective. The globalization era which evolved in the 1980s represented the intensification and deepening of the earlier internationalization processes and shared with them the notions of the interdependence of states and the importance of multilateral institutions and the rule of law. Its processes, however, were quickened and deepened by the technological revolution in international communications. In its particular form, globalization also promoted a different and narrower set of values. It universalized liberal models of economic rationalism, imposing on many different issue areas the same liberal principles of free trade, open competition, and transparency found in the international trading regime, but treating issues of social justice and welfare as 'externalities', or secondary aspects, of the international system.

After entering the principal international development and financial institutions, the World Bank and the International Monetary Fund in 1980, China embraced this neo-liberal economic model while initially paying lip service to its own revolutionary norms of social justice and welfare. In line with its continued opposition to domestic political liberalism and civil rights, however, it was loath to sacrifice its sovereignty by promoting the offsetting principles of international transparency, openness and accountability. By the mid-1980s, it had also in practice abandoned its declared support for social justice and equity. In refusing to use World Bank loans to finance social programs and social safety nets, and in insisting on the priority of economic development narrowly interpreted as increase in gross domestic product (GDP), it signaled to the world its acceptance of capitalist market forces as the ultimate determinant of China's new mode of development.[8] China's ratification of major international human rights treaties in the 1980s should be understood against a background in which it supported selected market values but in practice dispensed with its original social justice norms as well as the civil rights normally judged as critical to the smooth functioning of the market system.[9]

This selective acceptance of only the hard-edged aspects of globalization reflected China's lack of familiarity with the normatively richer and more equitable vision of Rooseveltian internationalism, and with the effective model of the welfare state in many Western liberal democracies. Its human rights crisis arose from the mismatch between the norms of globalization it embraced and the human rights expectations of its citizens. The latter were geared less to the values of globalization and more to the norms of socialism, giving rise to popular expectations that social justice would continue to be dispensed by an authoritarian, but ideologically disciplined, government.[10] However, contrary to such expectations, and in obedience to the dictates of the new market system, the Chinese government began to dismantle the 'iron rice bowl' hitherto guaranteed China's urban workers, thereby initiating a period in which access to housing, health, education and employment was to become a sought-after privilege rather than an assumed right. At the same time, the modernization of communications associated with the new market system brought a degree of liberalization of the civil rights of press, publication and movement, if not of freedoms of speech and association.[11]

The outbreak of China's Democracy Movement, which was the culmination of this clash between old and new values, and the government's decision in June 1989 to suppress it by force, proved a turning point in the relationship between China's leaders and the led.[12] Rather than opting to slow down the modernization and globalization process, thereby allowing Chinese society the chance to adjust more gradually to economic and social change, and rather than expanding popular access to human rights, as the students and workers had demanded, China's leaders chose to press ahead with further economic reform. Influenced by the free market ethos, they made a deliberate decision to pursue stability through the 'trickle-down effect' of economic growth, rather than through more egalitarian redistributive forms of economic and social development. They embarked on a move to downsize and 'rationalize' the inefficient state-owned enterprise (SOE) sector and to speed up China's accession to the WTO.

In exchange for the structural instability and human insecurity such a choice anticipated, China's leaders struck an implicit social contract with their people, to maintain an annual high growth rate of at least 7–8 percent in China's GDP.[13] This undertaking placed the government in a triple bind. The more social instability its international and domestic policies generated, the more the leadership clung to the globalization mantra of economic growth to prevent that instability and the more, in turn, China's economy became tied in with the processes of globalization. Any international development which jeopardized the operation of this remorseless treadmill by threatening the rate of economic expansion, whether it was international political instability, the outbreak of war, international recession or any other unforeseen international development was seen as anathema. The positive result of this was that China became preoccupied with the maintenance of international peace and security.[14] The negative effects were that, in deference to its new market-driven policies, it was now prepared to sacrifice social values which were not prized in the globalization stakes. The physical and social well-being of its citizens was now imperiled by new policies privatizing the provision of welfare and downsizing the workforce on the altar of hoped-for national prosperity. In its dealings with international organizations, China made the most of the advantages they brought of technical assistance, development aid and technology transfer. At the same time, it resisted the demands they made for increased transparency, openness and accountability.[15]

The second section of this article explores the consequences flowing from the timing of China's effective entry into the international system and the impact of its selective embrace of globalization on its human rights and international relations. Nowhere are the challenges of globalization more clearly demon-strated than in the effects of China's accession to the World Trade Organization (WTO), and in the outcome of its relations with the World Health Organization (WHO). For quite different reasons, its participation in both these international regulatory organizations set up a complex interplay between its human rights and its international relations, which highlighted the dilemmas posed by the developmental route it had chosen.

WORLD TRADE ORGANIZATION (WTO)

On December 11, 2002, following 15 years of difficult negotiations, China finally entered the WTO. No other organization has offered it such a volatile mix of potential costs and benefits. The significance of China's entry lies not solely in its impact on the WTO and on the globalization project generally: it represents China's most calculated gamble in the history of its entry into international organizations and its most unqualified leap into economic interdependence.[16] Apart from making sweeping concessions to the international community during its numerous multilateral and bilateral negotiations, it has also taken unprecedented steps to renegotiate the terms of its own sovereignty.

Why did China seek to join the WTO? International status, trading opportunities, the pressures of globalization and the desire to deepen domestic restructuring were all motives. The WTO was seen as an 'important carrier of globalisation', which would allow China to 'become a respectable member in the open international economic system', enabling it to enjoy equal trading treatment and to take part in formulating trade regulations. The WTO would have the crucial function of opening up China's service industries; it would link China with the global economy, 'bring about rational allocation of resources', allow more Chinese enterprises to operate outside the country and facilitate foreign investment in China.[17] Moreover, since China was not at that point a member of any regional trading bloc, it needed the WTO to remain competitive. Finally, it hoped that accession might improve relations with Taiwan.[18]

It is to be noted that these goals relate directly to the purposes of the organization itself. The WTO is primarily concerned with promoting, facilitating and regulating free trade. As the core organization incorporating, and generating, the values of the globalization era, it has treated the human rights aspects of international trade as 'externalities', much as the norms of globalization themselves do, and has relegated them to the oversight of the International Labour Organization. In like manner, China does not look to the WTO to address issues of income distribution or social justice. Rather, it utilizes its membership to pursue the social contract it reached in 1989 to maintain 'social stability' by achieving a high rate of economic growth. Accession has, however, obliged China to honor the WTO Understanding, that national judicial systems act in compliance with international treaty obligations and norms,[19] thereby, by implication, overriding Chinese domestic judicial decisions and practice. China has also become exposed to the WTO dispute system and to the courts. WTO membership has increased competition within China and will further erode central control over commercial policy. It has committed China to abide by the requirements of transparency, national treatment and non-discrimination. Membership has also required numerous policy changes, including significant reductions in tariffs, removal of no tariff barriers and quotas, the opening up of its service sector, further protection of intellectual property rights and the elimination of many barriers to trade in agricultural products.[20] It has required greater political openness and accountability. Moreover, under the bilateral agreement negotiated in November 1999 with the US, China made asymmetrical concessions in favor of the US.[21] In particular, the unparalleled, extensive and prolonged safeguards and anti-dumping provisions that the US negotiated were available to other WTO members under the Most Favored Nation (MFN) principle. Thus, Chinese economist Gao Shangquan distinguished four challenges that WTO membership poses for China: a challenge to the competitiveness of some Chinese industries and companies on the world market; a challenge to China's administrative system; a challenge to China's industrial structure; and a challenge to the Chinese government's macroeconomic control.[22]

However, the goals entailed in accession were related only to China's international political economy, its international relations, and the maintenance of its state apparatus.[23] The requirement of transparency in the WTO Agreement refers only to trade, as does the requirement of legal reform: neither benefits China's human rights. On the contrary, as Pitman Potter has observed, the effect of China's WTO-driven legal reforms has been to privilege market actors, the goals of social stability and central government control, rather than offering human rights protection.[24] Nowhere is the narrowness of the WTO requirements better illustrated than in the US report to Congress on China's WTO compliance a year after its accession.[25] Normally only too ready to scrutinize China's human rights, in this document the US government, observing the letter of WTO law, makes no reference to the human rights outcomes of China's accession and limits the critique of China's transparency and legal reforms to their trade implications.[26]

The effects of WTO accession, if problematic for civil rights, have been even more damaging for economic and social rights. These are now a critical source of concern, in view of former Premier Zhu Rongji's failure to create a universal social welfare system funded through investments in capital markets to protect the unemployed and other groups rendered vulnerable by accession.[27] Even the narrowly-based unemployment insurance system which exists in urban areas is beset with problems, as reflected in a 1999 Chinese report that 73 percent of households where the head was employed were not participating.[28] As Dorothy Solinger has argued, contrary to Chinese government claims,

> the 'win-win' scenario [of WTO accession] is only valid if the situation of a large portion of the 40 to 60 million urban workers in China who have already been laid off in the past half decade or so, along with the millions more to follow, is simply discounted altogether.[29]

WTO accession has created severe social strains and exacerbated the already crippling unemployment problem.[30] While the investment firm, Salomon, Smith and Barney, has predicted that as many as 40 million people (ten million of whom might be peasants) are likely to be thrown out of work in the first five years of China's participation, Solinger estimates that only 1.4 or 1.5 million new jobs will be created in the same period.[31] On top of that, according to a leading Chinese sociologist, currently about 140 million Chinese people live on less than $1 a day.[32]

For this reason, in the context of China's entry into the WTO on December 11, the World Bank's December 2001 report, *China and the Knowledge Economy*, advised China to create a minimum of 100 million jobs within the next ten years, particularly in service industries, for people moving out of agriculture and those laid off by state-owned enterprises.[33] The challenges China faced were also canvassed in detail in the 1997 report, *China: 2020*, which enumerated the following problems: China was one of the most polluted countries in the world; its spending on education lagged far behind that of many other countries; access to health care was declining; and social services were minimal.[34] As the World Bank Director for China, Yukon Huang, observed, 'China's economy looks like a huge giant perched upon a three-legged stool'. The three legs – financial reform, state enterprise reform and social protection – were interrelated, he contended, and could not be resolved in isolation from each other.[35] Major problems of 'urban labour adjustment' required new arrange-ments for pension and housing reform and health care financing. Income inequality and poverty reduction needed to be attacked.[36]

Given the privatization of China's health and housing systems that has coincided with the marketization of its economy and given the high degree of income inequality, the government's failure to establish a universal social safety net has not only undermined the economic and social rights of China's citizens but also represents a threat to social stability, the principal source of government concern.[37] Thus, China's new leadership, ushered into power in March 2003, listed the welfare of workers and peasants and the establishment of a working social security net as the priorities of its new policies.[38] It also publicized plans to extend to China's poor peasants the subsistence allowance paid to the urban poor and introduced new policies for migrant workers.[39]

Apart from its effect on China's citizens, the impact of China's WTO accession on its human rights has implications for the whole WTO system. As China implements WTO rules, it has met, and will continue to meet, numerous obstacles: problems of the inadequacy of WTO regulations to accommodate a non-market economy, including the inadequacy of existing surveillance machinery; problems of cultural mismatch between China and other WTO members, leading to differences in the interpretation of rules; the inadequacy of Chinese domestic financial and legal institutions; interference from, and non-compliance of, China's sub-national authorities; general problems of domestic implementation; and, most importantly, the danger that Western WTO members will engage in excessive disputation with China.[40] Thus, if WTO members place too much pressure on China, if its economic restructuring is pushed too fast and human rights abuses and social misery result, domestic unrest will increase. If, on the other hand, in the interests of domestic stability, China does not fully implement the reforms it has promised within the accepted timetable, it is liable to end up in constant dispute with other WTO members,[41] and globalization, together with China's international relations, will be the loser. At stake are two opposing variables, China's relations with the international community and the human rights of its citizens.

WORLD HEALTH ORGANIZATION (WHO)

China's relations with the WHO and its selective acceptance of its obligations have also created tensions between its human rights and its international relations, but in a different way to that understood by China's leaders. The consequences of this tension have also differed from the effects of its accession to the WTO. The global crisis which resulted from China's failure to report to WHO the outbreak of the SARS virus in Guangdong province in November 2002 has revealed the weaknesses in China's participation in international organizations, the flaws in its political culture and administration,[42] the parlous state of its health system and the deleterious effects which globalization has had on China's human rights. More than any other development, the outbreak of SARS in China has highlighted the close interrelationship between the well-being of China and the well-being of the rest of the world, to the point where questions of China's transparency and its treatment of its own people have become integral to global health.

In contrast to China's entry into the WTO, which involved a 15-year process of application and required the restructuring of Chinese policies and institutions well in advance of participation, its membership of WHO was the result of WHO's own initiative and did not require prior adjustment to the organization's norms. The Republic of China (ROC) had been a member of WHO from its establishment in the 1940s. In fact, Dr T.V. Song, China's delegate to the San Francisco Conference in 1945, had been the first person to suggest founding a single international health organization.[43] Although, soon after its establishment, the People's Republic made an effort to replace the ROC as the representative of China in WHO, as in other parts of the UN system its claims were rebuffed. However, following the entry of the People's Republic into the UN in 1971, WHO carried out the recommendation of the UN to recognize the PRC as the only legitimate representative of China. WHO membership conferred on China multiple benefits of access to health information, health technologies, and technical assistance. As a member, China was in turn bound by Articles 61–65 of the WHO Constitution, which obliged it to report annually on the action taken and progress achieved in improving the health of its people; to report annually on action taken on recommendations made to it by the Organization and with respect to conventions, agreements and regulation; to 'communicate promptly to the organization important laws, regulations, official reports and statistics pertaining to health published in the State concerned'; to provide statistical and epidemiological reports in a manner to be determined by the Health Assembly; and to 'transmit upon the request of the Board such additional information pertaining to health as may be practicable'.[44]

Like its membership of the WTO, membership of the WHO thus imposed on China requirements of transparency, openness and accountability. However, it was not until many years later that the full significance of these obligations was revealed. Two major and unanticipated crises – the global spread of acquired immune deficiency syndrome (AIDS) and the sudden development on Chinese territory of the acute respiratory disease, SARS – alerted the world to the fact that China had not yet made the necessary transition to an open and transparent system. These two human and epidemiological disasters were a potent reminder that China's response to globalization needed to be measured not just by its compliance with the rules of the global trading regime but also by many other criteria, in this case its readiness to disclose information on diseases which posed a potential global threat. Both health crises highlighted the fatal absence of transparency which was a feature of China's domestic political culture, and which, from the beginning, had also plagued China's relations with other international organizations.[45] They revealed a domestic political culture of secrecy and denial and highlighted the economic costs, as well as the costs to its national reputation consequent on such lack of transparency.[46]

China's failure to respond to WHO warnings about AIDS is well documented.[47] From the beginning, it denied the prevalence of AIDS throughout China, and, in ignoring the tragic issue of infected blood reinjected into the thousands of peasants who had sold their blood as a survival stratagem, lost years in a battle which it was finally forced to join.[48] This denial lasted from 1989, when the first case of AIDS occurred in China, until 1998, when it finally accepted WHO findings about the prevalence of the disease in the country. However, even by October 2002, the UN Secretary-General still felt obliged to warn China that it faced a looming AIDS epidemic.[49] The result has been that, by 2010, China will suffer from 6.4 million cases, and possibly ten million if the infection rate increases significantly.[50]

Despite the painful awareness that a swifter response could have saved tens of thousands of lives, China did not learn the lesson of the need for transparency and accountability. As early as November 2002, a businessman in Foshan became the first known case of the SARS syndrome, but, despite the continued spread of the disease, it was not until February 11, 2003 that China reported five cases to the WHO, insisting at the same time that the disease was 'under control'. By late February the infection had spread, via a Chinese doctor, to Hong Kong. On March 15, WHO issued an alert, calling the disease a 'worldwide health threat'.[51] Two months later, SARS had already spread to four continents, killing at least 98 people and infecting at least 2,400 others. On April 7, WHO Director-General, Gro Harlem Brundtland, criticized the Chinese government for not asking earlier for international assistance and, on April 5, the leader of a WHO team which had interviewed health authorities in Guangdong, dismissed the Chinese claims that the disease was under control.[52]

Having hitherto refused WHO authorities permission to travel to Guangdong, and forbidden the Chinese media to cover the story, on April 4 Chinese authorities finally apologized for not having warned the world of the dangers of the disease and promised to become a full partner with the WHO in its global investigation.[53] By then, 1,220 people had become infected in China alone. On April 15, admitting 1,418 cases and 64 deaths, Chinese authorities called the situation 'grave'.[54] On April 20, the Politburo Standing Committee warned against the covering up of SARS cases and demanded 'accurate, timely and honest reporting of the SARS situation'. Despite this, the WHO had still not been told to what extent it would be allowed to help contain the disease in mainland China.[55] Only on April 21, following the announcement of the sacking of China's Health Minister, Zhang Wenkang, and the Mayor of Beijing, Meng Xuenong, did a Chinese official proclaim that, on the issue of SARS, 'people's lives and people's health have to be put above everything else'.[56] A week later, David Heymann, WHO's chief of infectious diseases, admitted that 'China will make or break this disease'.[57] By May 8, China had sacked, suspended, warned or demoted 120 officials in 15 provinces for their failure to deal with the issue.[58] Rather than a sign of increasing transparency, the provincial response represented the traditional tactic of an authoritarian system which, apart from the sacking of two senior figures, followed its normal pattern of punishing the lower levels of officialdom. By May 12, 240 Chinese had died from SARS and more than 4,900 had been infected, the bulk of the world's total of over 7,000 cases. A day after the WHO insisted that it had still not received enough data on the spread of the disease, Premier Wen Jiabao warned that officials must take responsibility for the fight against it.[59]

The probability of a deliberate cover-up was suggested in early April by the revelation of a courageous Chinese medical practitioner that the official statistics supplied for the low incidence of the disease in Beijing were incorrect.[60] Of three military hospitals in Beijing, 120 patients had shown symptoms and three had died, while at a private hospital, there were 50 cases.[61] The cover-up had been achieved by a number of stratagems including, according to Jonathan Mirsky, loading SARS patients into taxis and buses that drove around Beijing and hid them from visiting WHO officials.[62] Apart from its political culture of non-transparency,[63]China's decision to hide the mounting crisis was most heavily influenced by its concern for its national reputation and the effects of a national epidemic on China's economic growth and tourism, fears of undermining the peaceful transfer of political power planned for the National People's Congress in March 2003, and even doubts about its impact on the 2008 Olympics. Thus, as a Guangdong official stated, 'Beijing has decided that SARS should be handled mainly from the point of view of safeguarding China's international prestige and credibility'.[64] The human rights of its people were very low on its list of priorities.

For WHO, apart from its fears of a global pandemic, the situation demanded awkward decisions about Chinese sovereignty. Faced with the outbreak of a few SARS cases, Taiwan authorities immediately requested WHO assistance and were rebuffed by the organization because Taiwan was no longer a member. Since the UN no longer recognized Taiwan as an independent country, permission was needed from Beijing to allow WHO to visit. Nevertheless, Taiwan responded rapidly, isolating itself from the outbreak, unofficially reporting information on its own cases of SARS, and receiving assistance from the US Centers for Disease Control and Prevention. The contrast between the responses of China and Taiwan led one observer to comment that,

> the lessons of SARS for China, and for the international community, are unmistakable. Democratic, accountable, transparent governments do a lot better at dealing with a health crisis than a communist one. Moreover, China's participation in international organisations does not, on its own, bring about responsible, let alone humane, behaviour.[65]

Subsequently, Taiwan's own crisis deepened, and China was obliged to give permission to WHO to play a direct role in its health outcomes, thereby implicitly renegotiating its sovereignty.[66] It also allowed five Taiwanese experts invited by the organization to attend a WHO meeting in Malaysia on SARS.[67] Because of the delay in permission, however, and because China had opposed Taiwan's annual attempts to rejoin WHO, Taiwanese President Chen Shuibian insisted that, rather than bringing China and Taiwan together, China's actions had 'widened the gap' between them.[68]

Paradoxically, the very results China's leaders most feared if they disclosed the SARS outbreak issued from their *failure* to disclose it. In this case, the costs were due not to participation in an international organization, as they were in the WTO, but to Beijing's inadequate compliance and cooperation with its obligations as a member of the organization. Even though China was declared free of the disease by June 2003, the effects lingered on.[69] Perhaps the most critical result of Beijing's lack of transparency was its impact on international public opinion, producing a widespread realization that the modernization and globalization of China's economy had not been accompanied by a change in its attitude. China's mistake had been to adopt perestroika (economic reform) without effective glasnost (openness). Domestically, the repercussions were also alarming. By early May, experts at the Peking University Economic Research Centre estimated that the disease might cost China 210 billion yuan ($25.4 billion) in lost economic growth, a figure equal to about 2 percent of its GDP.[70] The World Bank also estimated that China's economic growth had dropped sharply from 9.9 percent in the first quarter to 6.5–7 percent in the second due to SARS.[71] Subsequently, however, China's Central Bank Governor, Zhou Xiaochuan, insisted that SARS did not have a major impact on China's economy, which he predicted would grow by at least 8 percent in the first half of 2003.[72] Other assessments confirmed his confidence.[73] On the other hand, the uneven economic impact of SARS was now reflected in farmers' reduced cash income.[74]

Irrespective of whether the economic prognosis was optimistic or gloomy, SARS had a huge impact on China's human rights and created immediate problems of social instability. The neglect of rights was, and continued to be, played out in China's legislation. Despite the reporting requirement entrenched in Article 7 of the 1989 Law of the People's Republic of China on the Prevention And Treatment of Infectious Diseases, Jonathan Mirsky has revealed that, on January 23, 1996, China's Ministry of Public Health and the State

Bureau for the Protection of State Secrets had jointly promulgated a law according to which the 'highest level infectious diseases' were classified as 'highly secret', from the first occurrence of the disease until the day it was announced.[75] Somehow, this legislation, which both represented the political culture and entrenched it, had been slipped into the system as part of the allegedly progressive new 'rule of law', just as China was experiencing the burgeoning of an AIDS crisis. Thus were the seeds sown for subsequent disaster. Just as in the 1980s China treated AIDS as a public security issue,[76] so, in many ways, it treated SARS in 2003. Thus, on May 15, in a detailed legal explanation clarifying the Criminal Code as it related to the control and prevention of SARS, China's Supreme People's Court and Supreme People's Procuratorate announced sentences for behaviour hindering the fight against SARS, ranging from life imprisonment and even the death penalty for those found to have 'deliberately passed on infectious diseases', or to have 'jeopardised public safety', to lesser penalties for those spreading 'false information' and neglecting official duties.[77] In June, China jailed 180 Falun Gong members for allegedly spreading rumors during the epidemic, and launched a crack-down on China's media, shutting one publication and ordering an end to reporting on sensitive topics.[78]

The crisis also revealed the serious deterioration in China's health system since the pre-modernization period when its achievements in public health and other social services had been held up as a model by the World Bank.[79] It exposed the extent to which China had diverged from the Bank's own advice, which had explicitly warned it to avoid the privatization of health and education services.[80] In the new, partially privatized health system, the wealthy elite and state employees still enjoyed subsidies, while peasants were obliged to shoulder almost their entire health burden. By 2003, rural China, with 70 percent of the population, received only 20 percent of public health spending. The peasants' burden had become heavy, with the cost of medicine and health care soaring, and hospitals turning away anyone who could not pay.[81] Rural facilities were ill-equipped and staff poorly trained. Hence, on May 7, Premier Wen expressed fears about the possibility of rural migrants spreading SARS to the Western hinterlands as they fled the Chinese capital.[82] Compounding this danger was the cruel injustice that China's one million AIDS sufferers, the bulk of whom resided in the countryside, were believed to have a particular vulnerability to the disease. Growing concern among China's peasantry and workers also underlay increasing manifestations of social instability. Fears that the government would transfer SARS patients to remote villages, or that they would convert schools in urban areas into SARS hospitals resulted in at least four SARS-related riots by May 7. On that date, Chinese police rounded up 64 people for rioting in the northern city of Chengde, a city of nearly 4 million people northeast of Beijing, because they suspected a local clinic was going to be turned into a SARS hospital.[83]

Politically, the mishandling of the epidemic also engendered a severe decline in national confidence. As a columnist for the *Economic Observer*, Xu Zhiyuan observed, 'SARS has been our country's 9/11. It has forced us to pay attention to the real meaning of globalisation.'[84] An historian at Shanghai Teachers' University also commented that 'this disaster will make China's leaders more modest. Everything seemed to be going so smoothly, and that allowed us to neglect our systemic shortcomings'.[85] For her part, WHO Director-General, Gro Harlem Brundtland, drew the moral that 'the first and most imperative lesson learned from SARS is the need for all disease outbreaks to be reported quickly and openly ... in a globalised world, efforts to hide epidemics due to the fear of social and economic consequences will be truly costly'.[86]

As a result of this newly critical atmosphere, some observers questioned whether the SARS crisis might become China's equivalent of Chernobyl.[87] They suggested that it could have a transformative effect on China, promoting greater accountability, greater concern about people's health and greater administrative efficiency.[88] Certainly, the SARS development was empowering for the new President, Hu Jintao, who was seen as the main supporter of openness, in contrast to former President Jiang Zemin, who, in his capacity as Chairman of the Military Affairs Commission, had initially dragged his feet.[89] But, despite Premier Wen's statement at the ASEAN meeting in Bangkok that 'the Chinese government is here in a spirit of candour, responsibility, trust and cooperation',[90] it was more likely, in the light of the repressive measures subsequently introduced, that the new openness was primarily, if not wholly, an expedient measure to allay the immediate concerns of the international community. The Party's ability to cope with natural and man-made disasters and challenges in the past, without relinquishing power or increasing its popular accountability, suggested that SARS was unlikely to open up China in the way Chernobyl opened up the Soviet Union.[91] On the other hand, it was possible that the new leadership, under President Hu, might be prompted by this unexpected disaster to adopt a more innovative, bold and open leadership style than it might otherwise have done. The swiftness with which China reported a brief outbreak of the disease in 2004 supports this conclusion.

Nevertheless, the outbreak of SARS in China, and the failure to disclose the early spread of the disease to WHO, had multiple effects on both China and the international community. They revealed the full implications of the growth treadmill in which China had become trapped. In the government's view, the international transparency required by its participation in WHO threatened the viability of its social contract to maximize its GDP. For this reason, counterintuitively, the leadership was prepared to sacrifice the human rights of its citizens. In the event, however, the government's lack of transparency also threatened its primary goal of wealth maximization, China's international status and reputation,[92] and global human rights. The problem for China was that this issue did not lend itself to trade-offs. China's selective adaptation to globalization, and its unwillingness to accept its concomitant responsibilities of transparency, openness and accountability, had created a heavy burden, not only for the government, but for its people and for its relations with the rest of the world.

CONCLUSION

The polarity which has developed between China's human rights and its international relations has been a result of China's national choices. But those choices have been shaped by experiences for which the international community bears some responsibility. Because China was largely excluded from the influences of the international system for over two decades, its international experience has been relatively brief and largely shaped by the free market forces of globalization. Its preoccupation with economic growth and its selective uptake of the benefits and obligations of globalization in its relations both with the WTO and the WHO have undermined the human rights of its people. In the WTO, its single-minded pursuit of growth has meant that its international economic relations and its broader international relations have taken precedence over the human rights of its citizens. Yet, if human misery becomes so acute that China's workers and peasants rise up, as they are already doing in an unorganized and as yet piecemeal way, the situation will inevitably also have negative repercussions for China's international relations.

In the WHO, on the other hand, the effects of China's normative selectivity have simultaneously undermined both its human rights and its international relations. Within the international health arena, China's deliberate adoption of a policy favoring its economic growth and international reputation has had the contrary effect of undermining both goals. In no other global forum has the case for its greater transparency and openness with the international community been more compelling. In no other forum has the actual complex interdependence between China's human rights and its international relations been so clearly demonstrated. And in no other situation has the close connection between the human rights of China's people and the fate of the rest of mankind been so apparent. The costs to the international community of keeping China on the periphery of internationalization for over 20 years, and of obliging it to learn too quickly in a global international system privileging market values over human ones, have been onerous.[93]

NOTES

1. See, for instance, Gao Feng, 'China and the Principle of Sovereign Equality in the 21st Century', in Sienho Yee and Wang Tieya (eds), *International Law in the Post-Cold War World: Essays in Memory of Li Haopei* (London: Routledge, 2001), p. 239; and Wang Guiguo, 'Sovereignty in Global Economic Integration: A Chinese Perspective', in ibid., pp. 358–62.
2. See Ann Kent, 'China's International Socialization: The Role of International Organizations', *Global Governance*, Vol. 8 (2002), pp. 343–64.
3. Thus, it saw the establishment of the International Telegraphic Bureau (later named International Telegraphic Union (ITU)) in 1868, the General Postal Union (later Universal Postal Union) in 1874, the International Bureau of Weights and Measures (1875), the International Union for the Publication of Customs Tariffs (1890), and the international health offices in Havana, Vienna and Paris in 1881 and 1901. See Clive Archer, *International Organizations*, Second Edition (London: Routledge, 1992), p. 13.
4. Ibid., p. 14, citing *Yearbook of International Organizations* (1974), 15th edn, Brussels: Union of International Associations.
5. Jerome Alan Cohen and Hongdah Chiu (eds), *People's China and International Law: A Documentary Survey* (Princeton, NJ: Princeton University Press, 1974), p. 12.

6. See Susan Ariel Aaronson, *Trade and the American Dream: A Social History of Postwar Trade Policy* (Lexington, KY: The University Press of Kentucky, 1996), p. 3. See also Milton Churche, 'The Havana Charter for an International Trade Organization of 1948 and the World Trade Organization in Comparative Perspective', Economic History Seminar, Australian National University, Canberra, Sept. 7, 2001.

7. China was not denied all international organizational experience in this period. It joined or sent observers to the following communist intergovernmental organizations: the International Organization for the Cooperation of Railways; the Organization for Postal and Telecommunications Cooperation among Socialist Countries; the Fisheries Research Commission for the Western Pacific; the Warsaw Treaty Organization; and the Council for Mutual Economic Aid. For details, see Cohen and Chiu, *People's China*, pp. 1399–1401.

8. China adopted the 'trickle down' attitude to economic development, seeing growth as the only solution for poverty and social problems. Thus, China's Governor for the Bank, Xiang Huaicheng insisted that the World Bank and the International Monetary Fund (IMF) 'should help developing countries achieve stable and steady growth, which in turn will help reduce poverty and solve social issues'. See 'Statement by the Hon. Mr Xiang Huaicheng, Governor of the Bank for the People's Republic of China, at the Joint Annual Discussion, 'Statement by the Hon. Mr Xiang Huaicheng ... Washington DC', Board of Governors Press Release No 15 (Washington DC, September 29–30, 1999), p. 3.

9. Ann Kent, *China, the United Nations and Human Rights: The Limits of Compliance* (Philadelphia, PA: University Of Pennsylvania Press, 1999), pp. 42–8.

10. See Ann Kent, *Between Freedom and Subsistence: China and Human Rights* (Hong Kong: Oxford University Press, 1993), pp. 167–77.

11. Ibid., pp. 206–9.

12. Ibid., pp. 233–8.

13. Ibid., pp. 193–4.

14. China's four modernization goals consisted of the preservation of a peaceful international environment; maintenance of a credible nuclear deterrent; modernization of the Chinese economy; and enhancement of China's position in the international community.

15. Ann Kent, 'China and International Organizations', unpublished manuscript.

16. Kent, 'China's International Socialization', p. 355.

17. Gong Wen and Zhang Xiangchen, 'Comment on General Trend of China's Entry into WTO', *People's Daily*, May 7, 1999, pp. 1–2.

18. See Shi Guangsheng, Minister of Foreign Trade and Economic Cooperation, statement reported in 'China's Stance on WTO Accession Unchanged', *People's Daily*, March 13, 2001.

19. See Pitman B. Potter, *The Chinese Legal System: Globalization and Local Culture* (London: Routledge, 2001).

20. For instance, under the agricultural agreement, brokered in Washington in April 1999, the US won substantial concessions: the average tariff for agricultural products would be cut to 17 percent from 21.2 percent, with the average tariff for US priority products falling to 14.5 percent. All tariffs would be phased out by 2004. Quantitative restrictions, except for major agricultural products such as wheat, rice, corn, cotton and table sugar, would be eliminated. See Paul Mooney, 'Post-WTO Shocks for China's Farmers', *http://www.chinaonline.com/issues/wto/NewsArchives/cs-protected/2000/january/C00011721.asp*. Jan. 17, 2000.

21. According to US Trade Representative, Charlene Barchevsky, it 'secures broad-ranging, comprehensive, *one-way* trade concessions on China's part, granting the United States substantially greater market access across the spectrum of industrial goods, services and agriculture'. See 'Barchevsky on China WTO, Congressional Trade Status Vote', Feb. 29, 2000, available at: http://www.chinaonline.com/commentary, my emphasis.

22. 'Chinese Reform Expert Proposes Countermeasures for WTO Challenges', Xinhua News Agency, March 7, 2000; Reuters China News, March 7, 2000.

23. China's consciousness of the deleterious impact its accession would have on human rights, in particular, workers' rights, was revealed in a speech by Politburo Politics and Law Committee Chairman, Luo Gan, in which he underscored the Party's commitment to use China's legal system to protect against worker unrest and social instability in the wake of WTO accession. Cited in Pitman Potter, 'Are Human Rights on China's WTO Agenda?', *China Rights Forum*, No. 1, (2002), p. 9.

24. Ibid.

25. United States Trade Representative, *2002 Report to Congress on China's WTO Compliance* (Washington DC: USTR, Dec. 11, 2002).

26. Ibid., pp. 35–50.

27. See Economist Intelligence Unit, 'Financial Reforms Delayed', available at: http://www.chinaonline.com; and Premier Zhu Rongji, 'Report on the Work of the Government', March 5, 2000, http://english.peopledaily.com.cn/features/workreport/home.html. Only one person in ten is currently covered by social insurance. According to figures from the Ministry of Labor and Social Security, 150.77 million people of a total of 1.3 billion are covered by pension schemes. See 'Social Security Insurance Soaring in China', Xinhua Newsagency, Aug. 1, 2003.

28. See Dorothy J. Solinger, 'WTO Entry: Will China Benefit from this "Win-Win" Deal?', *China Rights Forum*, No. 1, (2002), p. 7.

29. Ibid., p. 4.

30. See, generally, *China Labour Bulletin*; Scott Greathead, 'Global Trade and Labor Rights: Uneasy Bedfellows', *China Rights Forum*, No. 1, (2003), pp. 27–9; and Erik Eckholm, 'Tide of China's Migrants: Flowing to Boom or Bust?', *New York Times*, July 29, 2003.

31. Solinger, 'WTO Entry', pp. 4–5.

32. 'Over 10 Percent of Chinese Live in Dire Poverty – Expert', Reuters News, July 10, 2003.

33. Carl J. Dahlman and Jean-Eric Aubert, 'China and the Knowledge Economy: Seizing the 21st Century', World Bank Institute Development Studies, Oct. 2001. According to the report, Chinese cities create 5.5–6.5 million jobs a year. But 8–9 million will be needed as many employees in state-owned enterprises and small rural companies, are laid off. The report also acknowledged that 'other projections estimate the amount of new jobs to be created at a much higher level – in the range of 200 to 300 million in the next ten years, due to the potential for lay-offs of half of the population currently working in agriculture, SOEs and TVEs', ibid., p. 16.

34. See also World Bank report, 'China: Weathering the Storm and Learning the Lessons', 1999.

35. 'World Bank Says China's Economic Challenge Mounting', *China Securities Bulletin*, June 18, 1997; Reuters China News, June 18, 1999.

36. The World Bank Group, The World Bank and China', *Country Brief*, available at: http://www.worldbank.org/html/extdr/offrep/eap/china.htm (accessed Nov. 8, 2001).

37. See Human Development Index (HDI) in United Nations Development Programme, *Human Development Report 2003*, available at: http://www.undp.org. China is ranked 104th in its HDI, in the category of Medium Human Development Level, behind states and territories like Turkey, Ecuador, Sri Lanka and the Occupied Palestinian Territories, but ahead of Vietnam, Indonesia, India and Egypt. On the other hand, based on 1998 figures, its Gini index, which measures inequality in income or consumption, is 40.3, higher than Vietnam's (36.2), Indonesia's (30.3), India's (37.8) and Egypt's (34.4). For recent unrest, see 'Chinese Steelworkers Protest Outside Beijing Government Offices', Chung Kuo Lao Kung Tung Hsun website, Hong Kong, Aug. 5, 2003, www.bbcmonitoringonline.com.

38. 'Premier Preoccupied with Rural Areas, Unemployment, Poverty', Xinhua News Agency, March 18, 2003.

39. See Andrew Batson, 'China Expands Social Welfare System to Include Farmers', Dow Jones Newswires, March 17, 2003; and 'Vagrants Get Aid as New System Begins', Xinhua News Agency, Aug. 1, 2003.

40. See Kent, 'China's International Socialization', pp. 356–7; Pieter Bottelier, 'The Impact of WTO Membership on China's Domestic Economy', Parts 1 and 2, available at: http://www.chinaonline.com/commentary, Jan. 3, 2001; Zhao Wei, 'China's WTO Accession: Commitments and Prospects', *Journal of World Trade*, Vol. 32 (1998), pp. 51–75; and Sharon K. Hom, 'China and the WTO: Year One', *China Rights Forum*, No. 1, (2003), pp. 12–19. For particularly valuable insights, see the proceedings of the conference, 'China and the World Trade Organization', Australian National University Faculty of Law, Canberra, March 16–17, 2001; and Deborah Z. Cass, Brett G. Williams and George Barker (eds), *China and the World Trading System: Entering the New Millennium* (Cambridge: Cambridge University Press, 2003).

41. Kent, 'China's International Socialization', p. 357. See also Bottelier, 'The Impact of WTO Membership'.

42. For excellent analysis, see Minxin Pei, 'China's Governance Crisis', *Foreign Affairs*, Vol. 81 No. 5, (Sept./Oct. 2002), pp. 96–109.

43. See Javed Siddiqi, *World Health and World Politics: The World Health Organization and the UN System* (London: C. Hurst and Co., 1995), p. 112.

44. See text of WHO constitution available at: http://www.wpro.who.int/public/policy/cons/_toc.asp (accessed April 23, 2003). The Constitution entered into force on April 7, 1948. Amendments were accepted by the 26th, 29th and 39th World Health Assembly (Res. WHA 26.37, WHA 29.38 and WHA 39.6) and came into force on Feb. 3, 1977, Jan. 20, 1984 and July 11, 1994 respectively. David Fidler has argued that, because the scope of WHO's International Health Regulations is so narrow, China had no obligation under Art. 2 of the Constitution to report the

SARS outbreak to WHO or any other state. See David P. Fidler, 'SARS and International Law', *ASIL Insights*, April 2003, available at: http://www.asil.org/insights/insigh101.htm (accessed May 19, 2003). However, according to Don Greig, a case can be made out that the functions of the Organization under Art. 2 to act as the directing and coordinating authority on international health work are so broad that it would be impossible for the Organization to carry out those functions effectively unless there were an implied obligation upon member states to keep it informed of all major national developments relevant to its mandate.

45. Kent, 'China and International Organizations'.
46. Joseph Kahn, 'China Discovers Medical Secrecy is Expensive', *New York Times*, April 13, 2003
47. See, for instance, Bates Gill, Jennifer Chang and Sarah Palmer, 'China's HIV Crisis', *Foreign Affairs*, Vol. 80, No. 2 (March/April 2002), pp. 96–210.
48. See Elisabeth Rosenthal, 'AIDS Scourge in Rural China Leaves Villages of Orphans', *New York Times*, Aug. 25, 2002; Elisabeth Rosenthal, 'China Frees AIDS Activist After Month of Outcry', *New York Times*, Sept. 21, 2002; Nicholas D. Kristof, 'China's Deadly Cover-up', *New York Times*, Nov. 29, 2002; and Elisabeth Rosenthal, 'Despite Law, China's HIV Patients Suffer Bias', *New York Times*, Jan. 14, 2003.
49. 'Annan Warns China of an AIDS Epidemic', *New York Times*, Oct. 15, 2002.
50. Gill, Chang and Palmer, 'China's HIV Crisis', p. 97.
51. Denise Grady, 'SARS: From China's Secret to a Worldwide Alarm', *International Herald Tribune*, April 8, 2003.
52. Thomas Crampton, 'With SARS on Rise, China Disputes UN's Travel Warning', *International Herald Tribune*, April 5, 2003.
53. 'China Apologizes As WHO Tracks SARS Path', Associated Press, April 4, 2003, available at: http://www.jsonline.com.
54. Thomas Crampton, 'China Admits SARS is Spreading', *International Herald Tribune*, April 15, 2003.
55. Grady, 'SARS: From China's Secret'; and 'WHO: China Too Slow in Reporting SARS', VOA, April 7, 2003, available at: http://www.voanews.com.
56. Reported on *ABC Radio National News*, April 20, 2003.
57. Chris Taylor, 'The Chinese Plague', *The Sunday Age*, May 4, 2003, p. 6.
58. 'China Punishes 120 Officials over SARS – Xinhua', Reuters, May 8, 2003, available at: http://www.nytimes.com/reuters. This was said to be the first time so many officials had been punished over one affair.
59. 'China Pledges All Resources to Fight SARS', Reuters, May 12, 2003, available at: http://www.nytimes.com/reuters.
60. Rather than 19 people with three deaths, as officially indicated, the real figure was much higher. See John Pomfret, 'Doctor Says Health Ministry Lied about Disease', *Washington Post*, April 10, 2003.
61. Ibid.
62. Jonathan Mirsky, 'Secrecy and the Spread of SARS', *New York Review of Books*, reproduced in 'Review', *Australian Financial Review*, May 16, 2003, p. 9.
63. See Minxin Pei, 'A Country That Does Not Take Care of Its People', *Financial Times*, April 8, 2003, p. 19.
64. Cited in Mirsky, 'Secrecy and the Spread of SARS'.
65. Ellen Bork, 'China's SARS Problem, and Ours', *The Daily Standard*, April 4, 2003. See also AAP, 'Taiwanese Say WHO is Ignoring Them', *New York Times*, March 30, 2003.
66. Joseph Kahn with Keith Bradsher, 'China Allows UN Agency to Help Fight Illness on Taiwan', *New York Times*, May 4, 2003.
67. 'China Welcomes Taiwan Presence at WHO SARS Meeting', Xinhua News Agency, June 17, 2003.
68. 'Taiwan Leader Says China Talks Unlikely to Resume', Reuters News, July 4, 2003.
69. Joseph Kahn, 'China Has Quelled SARS, World Health Agency Says', *New York Times*, June 25, 2003.
70. 'SARS Batters Chinese Economy', Associated Press, May 4, 2003, available at: http://www.nytimes.com/aponline/business (accessed May 5, 2003).
71. 'News Analysis – How China Maintains Robust, Soaring Economy', Xinhua News Agency, July 6, 2003.
72. Bing Lan, 'SARS No Snag for Economy', *China Daily*, July 1, 2003.
73. Chris Buckley, 'SARS Does Little to Slow China's Growth', *New York Times*, July 11, 2003; and David Murphy, 'China: Roaring Ahead: Evidence Suggests that SARS Did Not Seriously Dent

Investors' Long-Term Confidence in the Economy', *Far Eastern Economic Review*, July 17, 2003.

74. See 'Refilling Farmers' SARS-Hit Pockets', *China Daily*, Aug. 2, 2003.
75. Mirsky, 'Secrecy and the Spread of SARS'.
76. Gill, Chang and Palmer, 'China's HIV Crisis', p. 110.
77. 'Supreme Court Announces Harsh Sentences for SARS-Related Offenses', *Interfax China Business News*, May 15, 2003; Bill Savadove, 'State May Impose Death Penalty for Spreading Disease', *South China Morning Post*, May 16, 2003, p. 4; and Joseph Kahn, 'Man's Virus Infects Town, Killing His Family', *New York Times*, May 15, 2003.
78. John Pomfret, 'Chinese Scandals Lead to Media Crackdown', *Guardian Weekly*, June 26–July 2, 2003, p. 31.
79. See World Bank, *China, The Health Sector* (Washington DC: IBRD, 1984). For summary of findings in this and related World Bank reports, see Kent, *Between Freedom and Subsistence*, pp. 160–6.
80. Kent, *Between Freedom and Subsistence*, p. 163.
81. Mure Dickie, 'SARS Thrives as China's Public Health System Flags – Greater Reliance on Patients to Pay for their Own Medical Costs', *Financial Times*, May 8, 2003, p. 12; and Taylor, 'The Chinese Plague'.
82. 'SARS Toll Tops 500, China Fears Growing Epidemic', Reuters, May 8, 2003, available at: http://www.nytimes.com/reuters (accessed May 9, 2003).
83. 'China Rounds Up 64 for Rioting over SARS', May 7, 2003, available at http://www.nytimes.com/reuters/international (accessed May 9, 2003). See also Erik Eckholm, 'Thousands Riot in Rural Chinese Town over SARS', *New York Times*, April 28, 2003.
84. Cited in Erik Eckholm, 'Spread of SARS Acts as a Rude Awakening for China', *New York Times*, May 13, 2003.
85. Ibid.
86. 'WHO Chief Says Need for Openness Key SARS Lesson', Reuters News, July 11, 2003.
87. Joseph Kahn, 'When Crises Strike, China's Leaders Adapt to Survive', *New York Times*, May 4, 2003.
88. Erik Eckholm, 'China Said to Take Two Weeks to Disclose Sub Disaster', *New York Times*, May 5, 2003. One straw in the wind was the disclosure on May 3 by former President Jiang Zemin, two weeks after the event, of a submarine disaster which had killed 70 Chinese crew members. Given that military accidents in China are normally cloaked in the highest secrecy, Jiang's revelation could have been related to a new leadership consciousness about the need for transparency.
89. Kahn, 'China Has Quelled SARS'.
90. Jonathan Mirsky, 'Containing SARS: The scandal over Taiwan', *International Herald Tribune*, 12 May 2003, at http://www.iht.com.
91. See also Pei, 'A Country That Does Not Take Care'; Mary Gallagher, 'Openness Isn't Enough: Globalization and Political Change in China', *China Rights Forum*, No. 1 (2003), pp. 20–24; and Eckholm, 'Spread of SARS'.
92. See, for instance, Joseph Kahn, 'Reticent China Undercuts Its Milder New Image', *New York Times*, April 18, 2003.

The Chinese Diaspora, Foreign Investment and Economic Development in China

ALAN SMART AND JINN-YUH HSU

Rapid growth of China's economy since 1979 has been a critical part of its increased global influence, much more so than have its increased military or diplomatic capacities. As Jiang Zemin stressed in a speech in 2001, China 'knows what it needs most is a peaceful environment in which it can develop its economy and increase its strength'.[1] Absorbing large amounts of foreign direct investment (FDI) has in turn been a significant dimension of this economic success, not so much as a predominant component of total investment, but as a facilitator of hard currency exports and source of knowledge about and access to global markets. By avoiding current account deficits and indebtedness through reliance on loans, China may also have been able to retain a greater degree of economic autonomy compared to transition economies in Central and Eastern Europe.

Alan Smart is Professor at the Department of Anthropology, the University of Calgary, Alberta, Canada. Jinn-yuh Hsu is currently an associate professor in Geography at the National Taiwan University.

Globalization is an intensely contested term, and even the existence of it as a novel phenomenon is widely criticized as dependent on hyperbole that neglects the intensity of cross-border exchanges in the nineteenth century and before.[2] We consider globalization to consist of the stretching of human activities and their consequences across national borders and around the world. The core processes of globalization are widely seen as involving the creation of a global capitalist economy, the stitching together of production processes in multiple nations (the 'global factory'), and the heightened maintenance of transnational ties by migrants and other citizens. A significant proportion of the increase in international trade can be traced to the return of China to the capitalist world economy, and it has become the most important location for offshore manufacturing for export to the developed economies. Both changes are closely related to the influx of foreign investment.

The source of the vast majority of FDI was from ethnic Chinese outside the People's Republic of China (PRC): Hong Kong, Macau, Taiwan, and overseas Chinese in Southeast Asia and elsewhere. Although Hong Kong and Macau have been part of the PRC since 1997 and 1999 respectively, they are still administered as Special Administrative Regions under the 'one country, two systems' formula.

It is particularly remarkable that the second or third (depending on which period is discussed) largest source of FDI, Taiwan, is officially still at war with the People's Republic of China regime. Ronald Keith (2001) has recently analyzed the contribution of the concept of 'strategic ambiguity' in maintaining peace in the East Asian region. While the concept of strategic ambiguity has a specific connotation in the study of American policy, here we examine the strategic and tactical use of policies and representations that can be understood in dual or multiple ways in a broader sense. Such deliberately ambiguous representations of practices and intentions have been of crucial importance for the PRC in issues relating to Taiwan, capitalism, and the nature of the 'socialist market economy' and thus has been critical in facilitating the absorption of foreign capital and promoting economic reforms. Despite its advantages, particularly in terms of domestic politics, leaving certain things unsaid and unclear has both facilitated and hampered foreign investment in reform China.[3] One result was that until accession to the World Trade Organization, FDI has primarily come from investors with a higher tolerance for the risks posed by uncertain property rights and a level of political risk that was difficult to assess. For various social, economic and political reasons, the risk-tolerant investors tended to be ethnic Chinese, particularly Hong Kong entrepreneurs who also had the advantage of geographic proximity. In addition, the sensitivity of economic dealings with capitalists in the early reform years made it easier to deal with investors who could be referred to as 'patriotic' Chinese rather than capitalist profit-seekers. The result was that various tax and regulatory advantages were given to ethnic Chinese investors, particularly the 'compatriots' (*tongbao*) of Hong Kong, Macao and Taiwan.

In this article, we will first examine the impact of FDI on China's post-1979 economic transformation. Then we will focus in more detail on how

FDI was absorbed into early reform China, examining the ways in which ambiguity was mobilized by both sides to deal with the incompatibilities between the political economic systems. Following that, we will argue that the patterns of transnational connections have been transformed by the maturation of China's economy, and particularly by the recent shift towards a knowledge-intensive, high-technology economy. The forms of transnational economic cooperation that facilitated the boom in labor-intensive manufactured exports have become less appropriate in the current situation. We argue that rather different patterns of cooperation (especially linkages based on education rather than kinship or shared native place) between Taiwan and Silicon Valley are being transferred into China's high-tech sector. These forms of transnational communities may be becoming more important as the earlier versions decline in relevance.

THE ECONOMIC REFORMS AND FOREIGN DIRECT INVESTMENT

Almost a quarter of a century after Deng Xiaoping's economic reforms, it is easy to forget how (counter)revolutionary it was for China to admit capitalist investment in 1979. At least at first, it was clear that the 'capitalist road' could easily be reversed again, with serious risks for its proponents. Tentative early versions of the Open Policy reflected the trepidation with which China's leaders began to flirt with the enemy. As a result, China's economic reforms followed a path of indirection, ambivalence and gradual acceptance of what previously would have been anathema.[4] The crisis of Maoism combined with the rise of Asian Newly Industrializing Economies to encourage the post-Mao leadership to permit elements of markets and capitalism while endeavoring to control them and euphemistically label them.[5] Early efforts were limited by size and place: petty production and commerce and special economic zones.

The locations of the special economic zones were strategically located in areas bordering Hong Kong, Macau and Taiwan and where high levels of emigration had occurred. Émigré Chinese investors could be portrayed as motivated by patriotism, and not just as agents of a capitalist system intent on suborning Chinese communism to its will. For overseas Chinese investors as well, motivations were often a complex blend of wanting to contribute something to one's native place, or one's relatives, and pursuing profit from newly open pastures.[6] For China, capitalism was the enemy, but one with which it seemed that some degree of accommodation was inevitable, or at least temporarily strategic for the longer term project of building communism. China's goals were both to absorb and to control foreign investment, and particularly to preserve central control over society.[7] The initial problems posed by apparently contradictory goals were reduced in part by relying on groups of foreign economic actors who might hold feelings of patriotism and obligation to China, and who often have economic cultures more similar to or at least compatible with those found in China.[8] By relying on shared expectations and practices, the need to rapidly transform institutions and rules could be reduced or at least delayed.

Reliance on foreign trade partners who were willing to go along with Chinese ways reflects an important point: that for most of the Open period, regulation has been more important than has liberalization. As David Zweig indicates, China since 1979 has continued a long history of mercantilist efforts to control foreign influences even while benefiting from them. In this vein,

> the Chinese state established an array of regulatory constraints whose goal was to help bureaucrats control foreign and domestic forces. Thus China's opening to the outside world was not a free-market one. Administrative units and legal institutions ... constrained the way domestic interests pursued global transactions.[9]

The conflict of economic pragmatism and political symbolism meant that much of what was being done had to be done at first in tacit rather than explicit ways. One result was that the system of regulation did not provide adequate support for the new practices that were emerging. In consequence the new practices could be done very differently from one locality to another, with results ranging from the corrupt and near-disastrous to remarkable 'economic miracles'. The transformation of China's economy involved considerable experimentation at the local level, followed only afterwards by formal changes to legitimate innovations that are judged by the central authorities as worth promoting. A great deal of local diversity of economic regulation has developed as a result. Strategic ambiguity operates at all levels in this system: between Washington, Beijing and Taipei; between foreign investors and government officials; between local governments and the center; between formal rules and informal practices. Ambiguity of the rules meant that bureaucratic behavior was only loosely constrained, and local responses to these opportunities 'facilitated the weakening of China's regulatory regime'.[10]

Regulatory uncertainty and political sensitivity towards following the capitalist road have over time been replaced by a much greater degree of routinization, beginning particularly after 1989 and formalized in the commitments undertaken by Beijing in return for being allowed to join the World Trade Organization (WTO).[11] These circumstances have also unleashed a much greater flow of FDI from North American and European corporations, and have reduced the advantages previously held by those pioneers who were willing to take the risks of uncertain property and political systems.

Utilized FDI between 1979 and 1999 amounted to a total of $307.6 billion, of which Hong Kong accounted for $154.8 billion, half of the total, and Taiwan for $23.86 billion (7.76 percent). In all, Asia accounted for 76.79 percent of the accumulated total, compared to only 7 percent for the combined EU countries and 9 percent for the United States[12]. FDI inflows started soaring after Deng Xiaoping's famous 1992 'southern tour' launched a new set of reforms. The quantities expanded from $11.01 billion in 1992 to $45.46 billion in 1998, and reached $52.7 billion in 2001.[13]

While the inflow of FDI is often seen as an indicator of China's successes, or of the potential of its domestic market, Huang Yasheng has launched a trenchant critique of the emphasis on FDI in China's reforms. He argues that the high levels of FDI recently achieved by China represent weaknesses more than they do strength.[14] FDI has come to play a very large role in the Chinese economy,[15] not because all of the foreign firms are:

> the world's best-practice firms but because they are uniquely positioned to exploit many of the business opportunities in China created by China's inefficient economic and financial institutions.[16]

With a gross savings rate of 41.76 percent, one of the highest in the world, China is not short of domestic capital, but domestic capital is systematically disadvantaged. Domestic firms often need foreign partners to export, to obtain foreign currency, even to be able to do business in other provinces. Banks are forced to provide capital to cash-strapped state-owned enterprises (SOEs) rather than potentially successful town and village enterprises (TVEs) and funds move from deposit-surplus to deposit-deficit regions. One of the results of this situation is that 'efficient but private firms are denied access to China's vast savings pool and are too liquidity-constrained to finance their business expansions'[17] and are forced to deal, often disadvantageously, with foreign capital. China is selling valuable assets at prices that are much lower than could be attained if domestic firms were free to compete. Furthermore, much of the recent FDI does not create new productive capacity, but instead serves to transfer assets from SOEs to foreign investors.[18]

Given this critique, we must ask whether FDI helps to compensate for some of these economic weaknesses or exacerbates them. At least until 1992, there seems to be evidence that the contributions were on balance positive. This can be seen particularly in the crucial areas of providing information about world market conditions and providing the expertise and contacts that facilitated the rapid expansion of hard-currency exports.[19] While current account surpluses and substantial hard-currency reserves may have provided buffers that allowed the delay of economically important but politically difficult decisions such as SOE reform, they also generated profits that attracted agents from throughout the system to press for measures that would allow them to internationalize. It also seems politically very unlikely that more radical domestic reforms could have been adopted first. As Naughton points out, 'growing out of the plan' fostered domestic constituencies that could pressure the state for further reform, and as Zweig demonstrates, produced internal competition for the permissions that allow localities to pursue foreign capital. This competitive process frequently undermined various central state controls as localities selectively re-interpreted rules to make themselves more attractive sites for foreign investment.[20]

Huang does recognize that Hong Kong and Taiwanese investors made contributions to China's rapid economic growth. In a backhanded compliment, he argues against positive evaluations of China's gradualist ('crossing the river by feeling for stones') reform strategy by asserting that China's economy managed to grow 'despite its massive institutional imperfections due to its developmental stage (underutilized human capital in the agricultural sector) and as a result of luck: the nearby location of Hong Kong and Taiwan'. Without its ties to ethnic Chinese capital, he says 'nonstate firms would have atrophied under the weight of the lending bias'. He also recognizes that the under-development of the rule of law inherent in the gradualist strategy 'would have deterred foreign investment if not for ethnic Chinese firms that possess relationship capital and cultural know-how that help foreign firms navigate China's murky business environment'.[21] Expatriate capital, then, took on a particularly crucial role in the early reform years, even if its significance is declining in the post-WTO era.

Some studies provide evidence that is less negative about the impact of FDI. For example, between 1995 and 1999 the share of labor-intensive industries in foreign-invested manufacturing dropped from 50.42 percent to 41.44 percent, while that of technology-intensive industries increased from 26.86 percent to 33.21 percent.[22] Taiwanese investors at first concentrated on labor-intensive production, but have recently been key actors in the rise of high-technology industries in China, as we discuss later.

Another crucial question concerns the extent to which investment attributed to Hong Kong can actually be considered to be Hong Kong capital. In the first 15 years of the Open Policy, a considerable but difficult to estimate proportion of Hong Kong investment represented disguised subcontracting for Western manufacturers who took advantage of the policy advantages and cultural skills of Hong Kong intermediaries. The Hong Kong corporation Li & Fung has taken this role to remarkable lengths under the more fashionable rubric of 'supply chain management'. At present, there is considerable discussion of the extent to which Hong Kong investment is in fact 'round-tripping': domestic Chinese capital that is relocated to Hong Kong in order to take advantage of various tax and regulatory advantages, as well as involving the laundering of the proceeds of corruption. The World Bank has estimated that as much as 50 percent of recent Hong Kong investment is actually 'recycled' mainland money. While others suggest that it might be as low as 20 percent, the existence of the practice is not contested. However, a parallel process has involved the rise of the Virgin Islands and other tax havens as large sources for FDI inflows to China. The Virgin Islands, for example, increased its share from zero in 1996 to 9 percent in 1998. In 2001, these tax havens were responsible for 14 percent of China's utilized FDI. It is uncertain how much of this capital is of Hong Kong and Taiwanese origin.[23]

While still very important, the role of diaspora Chinese has changed considerably. Hong Kong investment has increasingly turned to large-scale infrastructure and real estate projects, while the coastal provinces have become less interested in low-technology manufacturing and eager to take their place in the high-tech future. Enclave economies focused on export processing are being replaced with industries that focus on the attractions of the Chinese domestic economy as well as the sourcing of goods for global production networks. Hong Kong export-processing investment in particular is coming to be seen as a feature of the past: low-tech and unlikely to contribute to China's knowledge economy, exploitative of workers, despoiling of the environment, and frequently based on corrupt practices and cronyism. While perhaps suitable for transfer to the less-developed interior, the coastal provinces are increasingly setting their sights on what they see as the future: the current high-tech boom in China. As we discuss below, the nature of the investment strategies and enabling relationships are becoming quite distinct in this field, even as ethnic Chinese investment maintains its importance, particularly that from Taiwan.

THE CHINESE DIASPORA: OBLIGATIONS, KNOWLEDGE AND STRATEGIES

The main question that we address in this section is the extent to which overseas Chinese investment had different effects, as well as a distinct character, than did non-Chinese transnational corporation (TNC) investment. It has been argued that there is a distinctive and crucial synergy between overseas Chinese investors and local governments in the People's Republic of China, one not found to the same extent or in the same form with non-Chinese FDI.[24] Thus, the synergy must go beyond factor complementarities, one of the main reasons why foreign investors find China attractive (another is the potential size of the domestic market),[25] since these apply to both types of capital. Synergy is seen as residing in the specific skill set of Chinese investors (experience with labor-intensive exports to the West and with managing to achieve high quality and productivity from unskilled labor), cultural similarities and propensities (shared culture and language, ability to form trustworthy relationships, values of authority and hard work), knowledge of how to get things done in contexts of policy uncertainty while minimizing transaction costs, and industrial structures that tolerate higher levels of regulatory uncertainty and risk[26].

One set of evidence for the existence of differences is that Western TNCs tended to invest in the large cities, while Hong Kong and Taiwanese investors were much more likely to do business in the countryside, although generally in rural areas with good transportation linkages. Non-local direct investment (that is, foreign plus Hong Kong sourced investment) in the Pearl River Delta of Guangdong province had the effect of reducing regional inequality through the higher concentration of FDI in poorer counties.[27] Since poorer regions often had higher rates of emigration, the promotion of investment from ethnic Chinese outside China through social connections generates investment in poorer areas that might not attract much interest were it not for the linkages. At the same time, cultural familiarity and social connections made the establishment and maintenance of operations in rural areas much easier for Hong Kong and Taiwanese investors than it would have been for North American or European managers. These relationships often made it easier to overcome political and economic incompatibilities as inconvenient rules were often ignored or 'adjusted'.

Hong Kong and Taiwanese investments have generally been smaller individually than Western TNC investments, were typically negotiated at lower levels of the government hierarchy, more likely to concentrate on export-processing than on gaining access to the domestic market, and less likely to adopt a Wholly Foreign-Owned Enterprises model.[28] They also tended to rely less on carefully negotiated contracts and more on personal ties and constructing trustworthy relationships. In the uncertain regulatory environment of the early years of the Open Policy, such approaches allowed them to set up their enterprises more rapidly and with lower transaction costs. Guha and Ray have argued that most traditional FDI theory suffers from lumping together TNC FDI and those investments that come from expatriates. They attempt to demonstrate that in low-wage countries, particularly those lacking transparent investment environments, expatriate investors have advantages over TNCs in labor-intensive manufacturing because of their knowledge of both global markets and technology and local conditions, languages and cultures. By contrast, TNCs have their competitive advantages in brand names and sophisticated technology, and see FDI in emerging markets primarily as a way of breaking into domestic markets that are closed to exports and where licensing arrangements are too risky or costly to enforce[29].

Critics have pointed out a number of flaws in the synergy model. First, it tends to assume both the continuation of cultural commonalities and the power of shared identity to facilitate trustworthy business networks which can then operate efficiently with lower transaction costs. This culturalist position ignores internal differentiation among Chinese and takes identity as an unproblematic given.[30] Second, it assumes that even while social connections are used for business purposes, their basis in solidarity and commonality resolves the problems of conflicting economic interests. Thirdly, even if business ties are more easily constructed and maintained among co-ethnic Chinese, and even if they do generate effective and stable cooperation, the approach 'still risks oversocializing economic behavior that is rooted in business and technological considerations' and thus 'assumes that social relationships determine economic transactions and outcomes'.[31] While economic relationships are clearly socially and culturally embedded, markets and industries have their own dynamics that reward certain types of organization and practices and drive others towards bankruptcy and failure. In the next section, we argue that the shift from labor-intensive export processing towards high-technology industries requires different kinds of supportive social relations. In the remainder of this section, we concentrate on the first two problems with the synergy model, examining how the expatriate capitalist/local government interface is often tense and contested, requiring skilled balancing of conflicting demands in an uncertain environment if the potential benefits are to be achieved. Claims to patriotic duty or the need for kin or natives of the same home town to work together may be rejected tacitly, even when acknowledged explicitly. The conflicts and tensions generally go without saying.

Reliance on social relationships to organize economic activity is widely seen as important enough to warrant discussion of a distinctive variety of economic organization found among ethnic Chinese and sometimes known as *guanxi* capitalism, or more formally as a reliance on network forms of governance. Outside the PRC, the utilization of *guanxi* has been more commonly seen in a context of the desirability of maintaining flexibility and being rapidly able to respond to changes in market demand. However, it is clear that reliance on law or networks is not an either/or kind of situation. Networks can still be important where legal protections are reasonably unambiguous, and legal protections can be pursued when social relationships are the main source of reliable interaction. In certain cases, the availability of reliable rule of law may facilitate the development of *guanxi*, or at least a tamed version of it, rather than inhibit it.

Douglas Guthrie has argued that rather than increasing with economic reforms since 1978 as Mayfair Yang claimed, the significance of *guanxi* has actually declined during China's economic transition.[32] This discourse of the declining significance of *guanxi* is often linked to a critique of the earlier forms of FDI from Hong Kong. Shanghai sees itself as more organized and efficient than the rather chaotic practices of Southern China. The changes that Guthrie documents as a decline in the significance of *guanxi* may be better seen as representing more effective controls on blatantly manipulative forms of *guanxi* practice related to cadre power.[33] Guthrie's study demonstrates that in the urban industrial economy, *guanxi* practices that allow actors to go around the law and grossly manipulate institutional procedures are now more likely to result in reprobation and failure, but this does not mean that *guanxi* is certain to fade away. After all, *guanxi* is far from insignificant in Hong Kong and Taiwan; it has simply been domesticated in such a way as to be more or less limited by the rule of law and concerns of economic efficiency. Our argument here is that while strategies of reliance on personal relationships may not always succeed, neither are negative outcomes certain.

Economic governance in China has become much more routinized and transparent in the last ten years, particularly in response to the requirements placed on China if it wished to become a member of the WTO. Nicholas Lardy argues that the concessions made by China required substantially more liberalization than exists in many other low-and middle-income WTO members.[34] These new arrangements have reduced the advantages of those expatriate capitalists who have knowledge of how to get things done in uncertain and politically driven contexts, and increased the advantages of Western TNCs. Western TNCs are also seen as having crucial assets that are in short supply among Hong Kong investors: brand names and cutting-edge technology. Thus, the flexibility, tolerance for uncertainty, social connections, and political knowledge that Hong Kong investors used to be the predominant agents in FDI in China are becoming less important in current conditions. However, the reduced desirability and need for this kind of investment should not blind us to how crucial it was when China was only tentatively opening the door to capitalist investment. Strategic ambiguity may have largely given way to transparent and universal rules, but without the contribution of ethnic Chinese investors that could be portrayed as 'patriotic' rather than 'capitalist', the reform experience would certainly have taken very different paths.[35]

OVERSEAS CHINESE TECHNICAL COMMUNITY AND
TECHNOLOGICAL UPGRADING: SILICON VALLEY-TAIWAN
CONNECTION

The economy cannot be reduced to interpersonal relationships, as it is composed of multiple production worlds defined by product configuration, market principles and technology and production processes.[36] In other words, dense social ties cannot normally substitute for the sophisticated managerial and technological learning that is required to compete in a particular sector. *Guanxi* arguments tend to overlook these complex differences, although in contexts where institutional barriers to business operations are unusually great they may identify sources of competitive advantage. Nevertheless, we will argue that *guanxi*, rather than simply declining, would work in another way in knowledge-intensive industrial sectors. In fact, *guanxi* (or ethnic social capital) could lubricate economic transactions, only if both transacting parts possessed complementary assets.[37] Instead of focusing on the strength of *guanxi* in the Chinese business connection, it would be better to discover the new lubricating role played by informal institutions in linking entrepreneurship and talents in the knowledge-intensive sectors.

This form of cooperation is particularly critical in the current business environment, characterized by short product cycles, knowledge intensivity and network orientation.[38] High-technology industries are noted for the continuous refinement of their products, markets and technologies, and product cycles shorter than a few months. Rather than exploiting cheap resources, firms with competent business models are looking for qualified and skilled teamwork enhancing human capital. Moreover, independent enterprises today produce all of the components that were once internalized within a single large corporation – from application software, operating systems and computers to micropro-cessors and other components. The final systems are in turn marketed and distributed by still other enterprises. Within each of these horizontal segments there is increasing specialization of production and a deepening social division of labor. In the semiconductor industry, for example, independent producers specialize in chip design, fabrication, packaging, or testing, as well as in different segments of the manufacturing materials and equipment sector. A new generation of firms emerged in the late 1990s that specialize in providing intellectual property in the form of design modules rather than the entire chip design. There are, for example, over 200 independent specialist companies in Taiwan's integrated circuit (IC) industry alone. It is the global production networks, rather than the large transnationals themselves, that constitute the pillar of the world economy.[39] The deepening social division of labor in the industry creates opportunities for innovation in formerly peripheral regions – opportunities that did not exist in an era of highly integrated producers.

In the new environment, flexibility becomes the catchword for competitive advantage, and clusters of specialist firms are better positioned to enhance collective responsive capabilities.[40] The key to success in the rapidly-changing market lies in capabilities to identify the right people (know-who), and accordingly fix the right technologies and products (know-how), as more innovations are human-embodied and team-working.[41] It is the learning capabilities, not existing endowments, that constitute firms' and regional competitive advantage in the new economy.[42] Moreover, as Lundvall argued, the learning process involves more than purchasing technology, and includes social dimensions such as the absorption of tacit knowledge, which is embodied in technical staff.[43] No doubt ethnic ties and interpersonal relationships can facilitate collaboration, reduce the uncertainty of economic deals, identify key resources and recombine them in new ventures. Shared language and cultures can help producers, even those located at great distances, gather information about people, capital, and other resources within the community. Therefore, building up capabilities in identifying know-who in the cross-border technology learning will be a primary issue for a late industrializer such as Taiwan to meet the challenge of global competition. To a certain extent, transnational socio-technical communities provided the networks for Taiwan to tap into the high-technology hub in Silicon Valley[44].

Accounting for technical upgrading in late-industrializing regions is a contested issue. While some top-down accounts, such as that of Alice Amsden,[45] suggest that the developmental state and key big companies (national champion) should be put at center-stage in the process of late-industrialization, other accounts focus on global production networks and argue that late development benefits from its insertion into global value chains.[46] Both are partially true, but fail to take seriously the embedded institutions in trans-border connections between technologically leading and following regions. In fact, as discovered by Saxenian, Taiwan's links with the Californian technology hub unfold in several ways: Taiwan's companies recruit overseas engineers, they set up listening posts in Silicon Valley to tap into the brain power there, or successful overseas engineers return to Taiwan to start up their own businesses.[47] All of these possible links are established smoothly not only on an individualistic basis, but largely through the mediation of overseas organizations. The central and largely unrecognized actors in this process are a community of US-educated engineers who have built a social and economic bridge linking the Silicon Valley and Taiwan economies.

The development of a transnational community – a community that spans borders and boasts as its key assets: shared information, trust, and contacts[48] – has been largely overlooked in accounts of Taiwan's accelerated development. The social structure of a technical community appears essential to the organization of production at the global as well as the local level. It is a kind of community of practice,[49] a group with shared beliefs about technological trends and ways of doing things, and it has expanded unexpectedly across the Pacific.

The experience of Taiwan has demonstrated the possibility of industrial upgrading through inter-regional cooperation and the reversal of 'brain drain' in the developing countries. Rapid growth of the Taiwanese economy in the 1980s, combined with active government recruitment ultimately reversed the 'brain drain'. Lured primarily by the promise of economic opportunities, as well as the desire to rejoin their families and contribute to their home country, growing numbers of US-educated engineers returned to Taiwan in the 1990s. The Silicon Valley-Taiwan business connection was institutionalized in 1989 with the formation of the Monte Jade Science and Technology Association. Monte Jade was started in 1989 by a group of senior Taiwanese executives with the intention of promoting business cooperation, investment, and technology transfer between Chinese engineers in the Bay Area and Taiwan. Monte Jade actively promotes entrepreneurship as well: a reflection of the extent to which the Taiwanese immigrants have adopted the Silicon Valley business model. A special committee of the Board of Directors offers assistance to individual members who are considering starting companies regarding corporate formation, growth, and development. It also helps member firms with the flow of investment funds, technology transfer, and mergers and acquisitions.

In spite of ethnic ties that facilitate cross-Pacific technological cooperation, the technical community benefits more from integration with broader business networks. It is clear that the overseas diaspora helped transfer technology and business models back to Taiwan. It is particularly true that while the Taiwanese firms in both regions had to rely on ethnic ties with mainstream businesses during their embryonic stages, *guanxi* could ease information collection across the Pacific. Trust and reciprocity incubated from primary ethnic bonds and informal personal relationships facilitate cooperation between these regions, and broaden the scope of *guanxi* building. However, the key to sustainable growth resides in the complementary assets possessed by the transacting partners, Taiwan and Silicon Valley.

It is the transnational technical community that allows distant producers to specialize and collaborate to upgrade their capabilities, particularly when collaboration requires close communication and joint problem-solving. The trust and local knowledge that exist within technical communities, even those that span continents, provide a competitive advantage in an environment where success depends on being very fast to market. However, these highly skilled Taiwanese immigrants are distinguished from the broader Chinese Diaspora (or 'overseas Chinese business networks') by shared professional as well as ethnic identities and by their deep integration into the technical communities of both technology regions.

Trust is the key component created by *guanxi* to lubricate inter-firm interactions. However, even if *guanxi*-embedded trust does matter in the transaction process, we still have to distinguish trust incubated by ethnic ties from that bred by learning. In most cases, firms place subcontracting orders to other firms, even with close ethnicity or classmate ties, with a small volume in the beginning, and then put in more orders after reviewing the first ones based on merit. It is the transacting process that thickens the social fabrics, more than vice versa. In principle, *guanxi* provides the basic ingredients for the two regional ethnic communities to build up trust for business in the beginning. However, trust should be monitored to refine, and thus could develop to allow lasting cooperative behavior. Although these two types of trust cannot be empirically separated, they should be treated as different theoretically. *Guanxi*-embedded trust helps the cross-border firms engaging in initial cooperative business, but monitoring-created trust ensures the deepening of these deals. While we agree that *guanxi* and cultural affinity could provide the channel for valuable information, we disagree that interpersonal relationship itself would create a faithful collaborative industrial community. In Chen's terminology, in this context effective *guanxi* plays the role of lubricant which enhances the transaction, not that of glue which fixes the transaction.[50] We do not argue here that there are inevitable contradictions between social ties and economic rationality,[51] but that distinguishing between different forms of trust and their embodied functions in business activities is essential for effective analysis.[52]

OVERSEAS CHINESE NETWORKS AND HIGH-TECHNOLOGY DEVELOPMENT IN CHINA

The connection between Taiwan and Silicon Valley through the mediation of transnational ethnic-technical community is not unique.[53] As China promotes high-technology sectors, such as computer and semiconductor industries, two sources of overseas linkage will benefit development in the new sectors. One is the extension of Silicon Valley-Taiwan connections to China through attracting Taiwanese high-technology investments. Another one is repeating Taiwan's experience and building up Silicon Valley-China connections by recruiting back talented individuals. These two trends sometimes penetrate each other and constitute a triangle connection.

By the mid-1990s, a decade after Taiwanese SMEs (small and medium enterprises) first went to China, the majority of the cross-strait investments shifted from traditional sectors, such as garments and footwear, to informatics industries, particularly personal computer (PC) components and peripherals.[54] An acute labor shortage and relatively high cost triggered the emigration of Taiwanese PC industries, starting from the most labor-intensive and price-sensitive keyboards and PC mice to power supply units, and then to motherboards and monitors.[55] In undertaking cross-strait investments a series of governance and coordination issues was posed for Taiwanese PC firms. The first question was the location of the new plant. Most Taiwanese PC firms chose PRD (Pearl River Delta) and YRD (Yangtze River Delta) as their destination. In fact, the locale of Taiwanese investments, particularly those high-technology investments such as laptop computer and integrated circuit industries, has concentrated in the YRD region, as Figure 1 shows.

As China's entry to WTO became all but certain in the late 1990s, a number of Taiwanese investors started setting up new companies to be responsible for marketing on the mainland,[56] or at least split up the local marketing division from other departments in the firm's organization. The role of ethnic social ties benefited the collaborative projects between Taiwanese high-technology firms and their Chinese counterparts in developing new products and exploring new markets.

On the one hand, by subcontracting the major electronics groups in China, such as Legend Computer, helps Taiwanese SMEs to penetrate the local

FIGURE 1
THE GEOGRAPHICAL DISTRIBUTION OF TAIWANESE IC AND NOTEBOOK COMPUTER
INVESTMENTS IN MAINLAND CHINA

(a) IC Industry

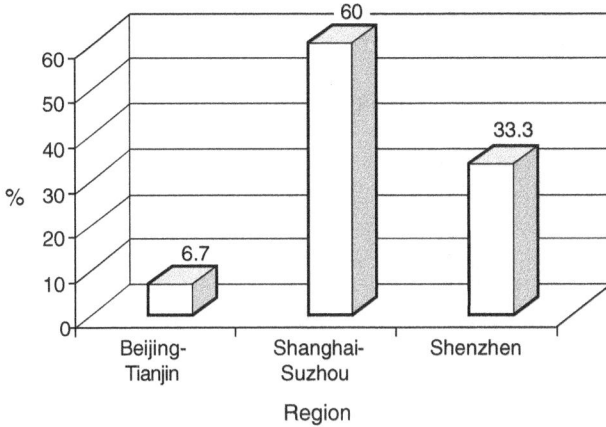

(b) Notebook Computer

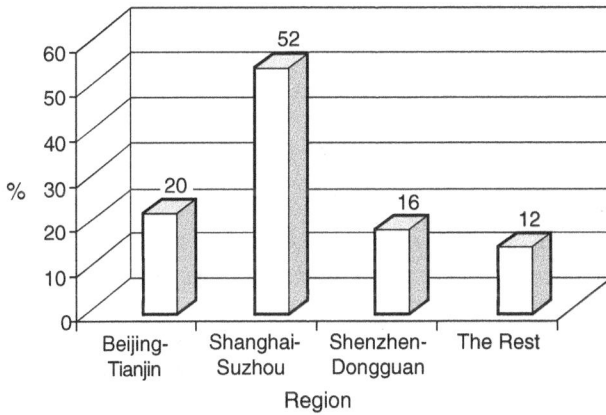

Source: Capital Business Group, *The Special Issue on Taiwanese Investment in China* (Taipei: Capital Business Group, 2001).

market, which appeared seemingly open but really maintained tremendous barriers.[57] On the other hand, collaboration could also extend to new differentiated product development, which might match the local demand. Take the collaborative project between Taiwan's First International Computer (FIC) Group and China's Legend Computer Group as an example. To facilitate the collaborative project, FIC sent out a team of several key engineers to Legend's new plant in Shanghai to develop new products such as notebook computers. In return, FIC established a stable subcontracting relation with the largest local computer group in China.[58]

Another famous instance was the joint ventures made by Foxconn Group with promising start-ups founded by local engineers to access the emerging product areas for wireless telecommunication, in which China's innovation base was believed to be more competitive than its counterpart in Taiwan. These investments were to target new product development, and to enhance the innovative activities for the Foxconn Group in China.[59]

The local market imperative is not just confined to Taiwanese investors' usual practices of playing subcontracting partners for key PC buyers, but also extended to envision the possibility of metamorphosing as own brand-name (OBN) makers with a high profit margin. Becoming an OBN producer was totally a new and knotty practice for most of the Taiwanese PC investors, who were well known for their hidden Original Equipment Manufacturer (OEM) factories in their global production networks. It required not only the production capabilities, which most Taiwanese PC investors knew quite well, but also the marketing competence, which included tacit knowledge about local tastes, specific standards, and exact regulations, to make a way into the long-protected China market. Besides collaboration with local customers like the FIC-Legend case, a number of Taiwanese investors had to recruit local talents who had better sales experience to run the newly-added marketing division. Acer Peripherals hired a group of local managers, including those who had spent several years in State Owned Enterprises, to strengthen its task force in pursuing the China market, according to Mr. Lee, the chief executive officer (CEO).[60] Inventec Group was also noted for its early establishment of local innovation teams to develop products (for example, translator appliances) and sell the products locally. As Mr Huang, vice president of Inventec (Shanghai) indicated, 'We had been OEM partners for key international electronics buyers for a long time. We could never dream of creating our own brand products until we arrived at Shanghai. But selling products in China was not a piece of cake, even though we Chinese shared the same culture. But the same culture helps us to identify the right people to take charge of local markets. So, we hired local qualified people with product design capabilities and marketing experiences to lead the division. They usually needed guidance in the beginning, but they could adjust themselves very quickly.' [61] After localization efforts, a number of Taiwanese investors started their own brand of products, such as Acer Peripherals who switched from a member of Acer group to BenQ brand maker; Quanta Computer, the largest notebook maker in the world, sold its products in the name of Getac in China; and Inventec Group promoted its Okwap cellular phones in the domestic market in 2001.

Together with capital flows, movement of engineers has become conspicuous recently. Due to political reasons, the central governments tried to restrict the flow of engineers either from Taiwan to China or vice versa, nevertheless, these restrictions failed in the end. Going to Shanghai has become one of the top options for Taiwanese engineering graduates recently, according to a manpower survey.[62] It was reported that SMIC (Semiconductor Manufacturing International Corporation), the largest and most advanced Chinese semiconductor firm, recruited over 300 engineers from the ex-employees of TSMC (Taiwan Semiconductor Manufacturing Corporation), Taiwan's largest IC firm, to Shanghai. It is believed that thousands of Taiwanese engineers and skilled laborers work in China. As China emerges as a source of cheap qualified engineers and an expanding consumer market, more Taiwanese high-technology firms will move parts of their operation inwards to exploit business opportunities. TSMC plans to set up its fabrication house in Shanghai, and will dispatch hundreds of experienced managers and engineers to transfer its operation. It is an open secret that TSMC would be the last of the key high-technology firms to invest in China, as others have moved in already. The expatriate managers and engineers typically travel back across the straits quarterly, suggesting that these firms continue to rely on their Taiwanese headquarters for strategic decision-making and direction.

While the Taiwan connection has been 'making capitalism' in China since the early 1980s,[63] a new connection with Silicon Valley has been emerging since the late 1990s. Many Chinese engineering students who studied overseas have graduated and worked for a few years in key industrial bases such as Silicon Valley. It was reported that of the 320,000 Chinese who studied overseas from 1978 to 1999, only one in three has returned home.[64]

However, as China's government targeted the development of high-technology industries, they provided many incentives to attract the 'patriotic' overseas Chinese engineers and entrepreneurs back to fill the shortage of experienced talent in the mainland. Under the efforts of central and municipal governments, 53 nationally recognized science or industrial parks were constructed to foster high technology.[65] These parks provided various packages of tax and land incentives to subsidize foreign investors. Among them, the Zhangjiang High Tech Park in Shanghai's Pudong New Area was paramount. Zhangjiang Park has emerged as a center of wholly foreign owned investment, which reached $3.4 billion in 2000, triple the average in previous years. This contrasts with joint ventures, which accounted for $659,000, and domestic ventures, which invested only $451,000. Zhangjiang hosted SMIC and GSMC (Grace Semiconductor Manufacturing Corporation), the two largest and most advanced semiconductor fabrication plants in China. These high-technology firms offer opportunities for returnees to combine their overseas experiences with local human resources. For example, the key role of technology development chief at SMIC is held by Mr Simon Yang, a Shanghai native who worked at Intel for 14 years. His colleague, Mr Joseph Xie, the senior director of marketing, also possesses similar working experience of seven years at Intel and AMD in Silicon Valley, and Chartered Semiconductor Manufacturing in Singapore.

Besides employment opportunities in large firms, several programs run by different levels of government agencies, such as the *Chun-hui* Program, grant financial and manpower support to returned entrepreneurs to start ventures in China. A number of Returning Students Venture Parks were established to target returning entrepreneurs. Combined with the perception of greater stability and the large local pool of cheap and capable engineers, these incentives attracted overseas Chinese students back. According to one estimate, one quarter of the more than 200,000 students who studied overseas after 1978 had returned by early 2000.[66] For example, more than 1,000 returning Chinese electrical engineers have settled in the Shanghai area, and they have founded more than 150 companies, mostly small enterprises.[67]

Similarly to the Silicon Valley-Taiwan connection, China's link was built on the individual level first, but soon became institutionalized by establishing a transnational community. A number of associations and groups were organized to enhance technical and social interaction among the members. At first, these organizations were set up in Silicon Valley, and later they were extended back to the mainland as high-technology infrastructures gradually became available, as has been well documented by Saxenian.[68] One of the key associations, the Hua Yuan Science & Technology Association, was formed in Silicon Valley in 2000 to: 'promote the technological, professional and scientific development of the Chinese business community'. Hua Yuan and other Chinese professional associations also sponsor regular business tours to China, receive government delegations, and serve as conduits for Chinese firms recruiting in the US. Through the fora provided by these organizations, two-way channels were established for Silicon Valley's high-technology capital and China's emerging market and manpower.

However, as demonstrated by the case of Hua Yuan, the immigrant engineers from mainland China, a fast-growing presence in Silicon Valley in the 1990s, are creating their own social and professional associations rather than joining those established by their Taiwanese predecessors, such as Monte Jade. This divide underscores the dangers of overstating the power of race or nationality in creating cohesive ethnic identities, which is often taken for granted in discussions of the business networks of the Overseas Chinese. Collective identities are constructed over time, often through the kinds of face-to-face social interactions that are facilitated by geographic, occupational, or industrial concentration. Initial social connections often have a basis in shared educational experiences, technical backgrounds, language, culture and history. Once established, these concentrations promote the frequent, intensive interactions that breed a sense of commonality and identification with members of the same group – and at the same time, exclude others, even of similar racial characteristics.

But we should not hastily conclude that Silicon Valley, today's pre-eminent high-technology hub, has distinctly separate connections with China and Taiwan, as they ultimately share similar technical and business interests. The emergence of the China-Silicon Valley connection also facilitates the cross-penetration between these overseas Taiwanese and Chinese associations; some of them were even initiated by the ostensibly opposed governments on either side of the Taiwan Strait. Despite the rejection of Monte Jade's application to set up a branch office in Beijing by China's government, Monte Jade invited one senior mainland Chinese entrepreneur to join its steering committee. In fact, regardless of political differences, overseas Chinese entrepreneurs who originated from Taiwan are eager to introduce the Silicon Valley model to mainland China, as they see tremendous business opportunities there. The list of investors is largely the same as that in early Taiwan-Silicon Valley linkages.[69] In most cases, the cross-Pacific collaboration would involve not only the capital and technology sending and receiving points (Silicon Valley and China respectively), but also an intermediary role played by Taiwan's high-technology investors.

The case of Acorn Campus is particularly illustrative here. The Campus was mainly established by a team of successful Taiwanese venture capitalists and engineers based in Silicon Valley. It plans to introduce the incubator model to Shanghai and focuses on semiconductor design, wireless infrastructure, and system and software development. It aims to exploit the best resources from different locations: research and development (R & D), new product development and marketing in the US, high-end logistics, design and manufacturing in Taiwan, and low-cost engineering and manufacturing talent in China.[70] Another good example is the case of WI Harper, a venture capital company registered in Silicon Valley with major funds sourced from Taiwan. It assembled a new fund of about $30 million in 2001, and allocated 20 percent in Taiwan, 30 percent in China and 50 percent in Silicon Valley to develop new products in biotechnology. By doing so, it will be able to mobilize a variety of talents through high-technology business networks.

In other words, a triangle connection between Silicon Valley-Taiwan-China is emerging and creates a pattern of capital and brain circulation in the nodes of transnational business networks. The power of the transnational technical community is evident, and has become a key force in shaping the global production networks. It originated in Silicon Valley and has been transferred by overseas Chinese (emigrated from Taiwan) entrepreneurs first to Taiwan and then from Taiwan as well as directly from Silicon Valley to China. The dense social and professional networks foster multivarious flows of technology, capital, know-how, and information within the triangle, supporting entrepreneurship in the three regions while also providing the foundation for formal inter-regional business relations such as consortia, joint ventures, and partnerships.

CONCLUDING REMARKS

We have argued in this paper that the availability of overseas Chinese capital was an important element of China's effective reincorporation into the global economy. The availability of large populations possessing investment capital and expertise in labor-intensive production and export markets who were willing to accept high levels of risk and uncertainty was a key advantage in China's reform strategy. It allowed them to maintain a high level of strategic ambiguity in a period when collaboration with capitalism was a profoundly contested approach while still enabling capitalist production that could be competitive on world markets. This in turn allowed trade surpluses and foreign currency reserves that enabled Beijing to mollify powerful sectors such as the SOEs and the People's Liberation Army through investment in modernization. The characteristics of overseas Chinese FDI have been quite different from those of investments by TNCs, and arguably more appropriate for the needs of early reform China.

We have also argued here, however, that the utilities provided by socially connected expatriate investment in the early reform period have become less necessary and even less useful as the reforms have matured and become more systematic, particularly during the transition to WTO membership. China's ambitions in the high-technology sectors in particular have highlighted the need for different patterns of FDI absorption. Our comparison between the Taiwan-Silicon Valley linkages and the triangular transnational technical community, that is starting to emerge through bringing mainland China into the mix, provides new perspectives on the role of *guanxi* and strategic ambiguity in expatriate-sourced FDI and China's current developmental dynamics.

Firstly, strategic ambiguity was not just exploited by China's government towards Taiwan and capitalism, but was also conversely used by the overseas Chinese technical community, particularly those originating from Taiwan, to take advantage of the asset mobilization in China. The case of the early exclusiveness of Monte Jade demonstrated that kin and native place ties are not always useful as lubricants in business transactions. Their efficacy depends on the broader social contexts and economic opportunities. The final collaboration between the Taiwanese-origin Monte Jade and the mainlander-initiated Hua Yuan illustrates that the emergence of an overseas Chinese technical community could be possible only under the condition of complementary assets among the triangle regions. It is particularly true as China's large potential market will provide local producers with the opportunity to experiment with, and ultimately innovate, in the field of high-technology industries such as wireless communications.

Secondly, the role played by ethnic ties in the high-technology sectors differs from what has been widely described in labor-intensive industries. Rather than arguing that ethnic social capital will not work in the technology-intensive industries, we contend that its role and style is changed. Ethnic social capital was crucial for reducing transaction costs (or indeed even making investment possible at all in certain circumstances) and enhancing mutual trust in the early stages of overseas Chinese investments in mainland China., After the business environment became clearer and technology-intensive investment became more sought-after, ethnic ties became more important as collective assets which assisted in the identification and recruitment of appropriate talents among overseas Chinese in the United States and across the Taiwan Strait. In other word, such ethnic social ties, rather than simply exploiting the opportunities of a context of transitional chaos combined with large factor complementarities, have come to fulfill the need of 'know-who' in the learning economy in which the social dimension is the key and often-ignored issue in the constitution of competitiveness.[71]

Thirdly, the kind of social ties that are of greatest strategic importance in the high-tech sectors are no longer those founded upon kinship and home town ties.

Close relatives are unlikely to have the specific knowledge and skills that are needed to be at the cutting edge of technological competition. Instead, the right links are more likely to be found through the weak ties among classmates and joint membership in technological associations. While initially not offering the same degree of trust afforded by strong ties, trusted relationships can be built through the processes of cooperating in small ways first and learning who can be trusted and how they can be worked with. Again, it seems to us a remarkable thing that, in the absence of diplomatic ties between Taiwan and mainland China and when non-governmental organizations are still treated with distrust by Beijing, associations that bring together the two sides of the Taiwan Strait and Silicon Valley are managing to foster a fledgling, inclusive, transnational, and technical community. Thus, although strategic ambiguity has been transformed by the routinization of the Chinese business environment, it still serves some critically important roles at present and into the foreseeable future.

NOTES

1. Quoted in Ronald C. Keith, ' "Strategic Ambiguity" and the new Bush Administration's "China Threat"', *The Review of International Affairs*, Vol. 1, No. 2 (Winter 2001), pp. 1–19.
2. See, for example, Sidney Mintz, 'The Localization of Anthropological Practice: From Area Studies to Transnationalism', *Critique of Anthropology*, Vol. 18 (1998), pp. 117–33; and P. Hirst and G. Thompson, *Globalization in Question* (Cambridge, MA: Polity Press, 1996).
3. Alan Smart and Josephine Smart, 'Transnational Social Networks and Negotiated Identities in Interactions between Hong Kong and China', in Michael Peter Smith and Luis Eduardo Guarnizo, *Transnationalism from Below* (New Brunswick, NJ: Transaction Publishers, 1998), pp. 103–29. This usage draws on a long tradition of ethnographic examination of the strategic use of ambiguity in social interaction, see for example, Pierre Bourdieu, *Outline of a Theory of Practice* (Cambridge: Cambridge University Press, 1977); and F.G. Bailey, *The Prevalence of Deceit* (Ithaca, NY: Cornell University Press, 1991).
4. Josephine Smart and Alan Smart, 'Personal Relations and Divergent Economies: a Case Study of Hong Kong investment in China', *International Journal of Urban and Regional Research*, 15 (1991), pp. 216–33. See also Margaret M. Pearson, *Joint Ventures in the People's Republic of China* (Princeton, NJ: Princeton University Press, 1991); and Dorothy S. Solinger, *Chinese Business Under Socialism* (Berkeley, CA: University of California Press, 1984).
5. Alan Smart,' Oriental despotism and sugar-coated bullets: Representations of the Market in China', in James Carrier, *Meanings of the Market: The Free Market in Western Culture* (Oxford: Berg, 1997), pp. 159–94.
6. Laurence J.C. Ma, 'Space, place and transnationalism in the Chinese diaspora', in Laurence J.C. Ma and Carolyn Cartier, *The Chinese Diaspora: Space, Place, Mobility, and Identity* (Lanham, MD: Rowman & Littlefield, 2002), p. 28.
7. Pearson, *Joint Ventures*, p. 4; Pitman B. Potter 'Foreign Investment Law in the People's Republic of China: Dilemmas of State Control', *The China Quarterly*, Vol. 141 (1995), pp. 155–85.
8. Hsing You-tien, *Making Capitalism in China: The Taiwan Connection* (New York: Oxford University Press, 1998); Tseng Yen-fen 'From "us" to "them": Diasporic Linkages and Identity Politics', *Identities*, Vol. 9, No. 3 (July-Sept. 2002), pp. 383–404; Chen Xiangming, 'Both glue and lubricant: Transnational Ethnic Social Capital as a Source of Asia-Pacific Subregionalism', *Policy Sciences*, Vol. 33 (2000), pp. 269–87.
9. David Zweig, *Internationalizing China: Domestic Interests and Global Linkages* (Ithaca, NY: Cornell University Press, 2002), p. 31.
10. Ibid., p. 88.
11. Nicholas R. Lardy, *Integrating China into the Global Economy* (Washington DC: Brookings Institution Press, 2002).

12. Ministry of Foreign Trade and Economic Cooperation (MOFTEC), available at: http://www.moftec.gov.cn. Below, whenever statistics on FDI are cited without attribution to a different source, they are obtained from MOFTEC.
13. Chen Chunlai, 'Foreign Direct Investment: Prospects and Policies', in *China in the World Economy: The Domestic Policy Challenges* (Paris: OECD, 2002), p. 324.
14. Huang Yasheng, *Selling China: Foreign Direct Investment during the Reform Era* (Cambridge: Cambridge University Press, 2003).
15. The ratio of FDI to gross fixed capital between 1992 and 1998 was 13.1 percent for China compared to 6.9 percent for the United States. See Huang, *Selling China*, p. 13.
16. Huang Yasheng, 'Internal and External Reforms: Experiences and Lessons from China', *Cato Journal*, Vol. 21, No. 1 (Spring/Summer 2001), p. 54. In a parallel critique, it has been argued that China has been an underachiever in attracting FDI from the main source countries such as the US, instead relying on Hong Kong *et al.* See Wei Shang-Jin, 'Why does China attract so little foreign direct investment?', in T. Ito and A.O. Krueger, *The Role of Foreign Direct Investment in East Asian Economic Development* (Chicago, IL: University of Chicago Press, 2000), pp. 230–61.
17. Huang, 'Internal and External Reforms', p. 58.
18. This process can be seen as a variant of asset stripping prevalent in China's privatization, see Ding Xueling, 'Who gets what, how? When Chinese State-Owned Enterprises become Shareholding Companies', *Problems of Post-Communism*, Vol. 46, No. 3, 1999, pp. 32–41.
19. Huang, *Selling China*, p. 18.
20. Barry Naughton, *Growing Out of the Plan: Chinese Economic Reform, 1978–1993* (New York: Cambridge University Press, 1995); and Zweig, *Internationalizing China*
21. Huang, 'Internal and External Reforms', p. 62.
22. Chen Chunlai, 'Foreign Direct Investment', p. 329.
23. Dilek Aykut and Dilip Ratha, 'South-south FDI flows in the 1990s', background paper for Global Development Finance, World Bank, April 3, 2002, p. 18; The United States-China Business Council, March 2002, available at: http://www.uschina.org/statistics/03-01.html. For a broader discussion of the accounting issues at stake, see Linda Low, Eric D. Ramstetter and Henry Wai-Chung Yeung, 'Accounting for Outward Direct Investment from Hong Kong and Singapore: Who Controls What?', in Robert E. Baldwin, Robert E. Lipsey and J. David Richardson, *Geography and Ownership as Bases for Economic Accounting* (Chicago, IL: University of Chicago Press, 1998), pp. 139–71.
24. Constance Lever-Tracy, David Ip and Noel Tracy, *The Chinese Diaspora and Mainland China: An Emerging Economic Synergy* (Houndmills: Macmillan Press, 1996); Brad Christerson and Constance Lever-Tracy, 'The Third China? Emerging Industrial Districts in Rural China', *International Journal of Urban and Regional Research*, Vol. 21, No. 4 (1997), pp. 569–88; George C.S. Lin, *Red Capitalism in South China: Growth and Development of the Pearl River Delta* (Vancouver, BC: University of British Columbia Press, 1997).
25. Huang Yasheng argues that these explanations for FDI based on investor motivations are inadequate since they do not account as to why domestic firms do not compete for the same opportunities. See Huang, *Selling China*, p. 42.
26. Alan Smart and Josephine Smart, 'Failures and Strategies of Hong Kong Firms in China: An Ethnographic Perspective', in Henry Wai-Chung Yeung and Kris Olds, *Globalisation of Chinese Business Firms* (London: Macmillan, 2000), pp. 244–71; Henry Wai-Chung Yeung, 'Local Politics and Foreign Ventures in China's Transitional Economy: the Political Economy of Singaporean Investments in China', *Political Geography*, Vol. 19 (2000), pp. 809–40; and Hsing, *Making Capitalism in China*.
27. Jianfa Shen, Kwan-yiu Wong and David K.Y. Chu, 'Regional economic growth and factor contributions in the Zhujiang Delta Region of south China', *Asian Geographer*, Vol. 20 (2001), pp. 125–51.
28. Smart and Smart, 'Personal Relations'; Zweig *Internationalizing China*; and Shi Yi-zheng, Ho Po-yuk and Siu Wai-sum, 'Market Entry Mode Selection: The Experience of Small Hong Kong Firms Investing in China', *Asia-Pacific Business Review*, Vol. 8, No. 1 (Autumn 2001), pp. 19–41.
29. Ashok S. Guha and Amit S. Ray, 'Expatriate vs. Multinational Investment: A Comparative Analysis of their Roles in Chinese and Indian Development', paper presented at the 'WTO, China and the Asian Economies' conference, Beijing, Nov. 2002. Their analysis found that expatriate Chinese have been able to have more impact on economic development in China than in India.

30. Tseng, 'Diasporic Linkages'; Hsing You-tien, 'Ethnic Identity and Business Solidarity: Chinese Capitalism Revisited', in Laurence J.C. Ma and Carolyn Cartier, *The Chinese Diaspora: Space, Place, Mobility, and Identity* (Lanham, MD: Rowman & Littlefield, 2002), pp. 221–35; Alan Smart and Josephine Smart, 'Transnational Social Networks and Negotiated Identities in Interactions Between Hong Kong and China', in Michael Peter Smith and Luis E. Guarnizo, *Transnationalism From Below* (New Brunswick, NJ: Transaction Publishers, 1998), pp. 103–29.

31. Hsu Jinn-yuh and AnnaLee Saxenian, 'The Limits of *Guanxi* Capitalism: Transnational Collaboration between Taiwan and the USA', *Environment and Planning A*, Vol. 32 (2000), p. 1994.

32. Douglas Guthrie, 'The Declining Significance of *Guanxi* in China's Economic Transition', *The China Quarterly*, Vol. 154 (1998), pp. 254–82; Mayfair Yang, *Gifts, Favors and Banquets: The Art of Social Relationships in China* (Ithaca, NY: Cornell University Press, 1994); Mayfair Yang 'The Resilience of *Guanxi* and its New Deployments: A Critique of Some New *Guanxi* Scholarship', *The China Quarterly*, Vol. 170 (June 2002), pp. 459–76; and Smart and Smart 'Failures and Strategies'.

33. His research relied on formal questionnaires administered to employees in SOEs and joint ventures, with a resulting normative bias against the acknowledgment of the respondent's reliance on *guanxi*.

34. Lardy, *Integrating China*.

35. For a discussion of how China has reinterpreted 'patriotism' to encourage overseas Chinese to contribute to the building of the nation, see Pal Nyiri, 'Expatriating is patriotic? The discourse on 'new migrants' in the People's Republic of China and identity construction among recent migrants from the PRC', *Journal of Ethnic and Migration Studies*, Vol. 27, No. 4 (Oct. 2001), pp. 635–53.

36. Michael Storper and Robert Salais, *Worlds of Production: The Action Frameworks of the Economy* (Cambridge, MA: Harvard University Press, 1997).

37. Chen/Xiangming, 'Both glue and lubricant' (2000).

38. Manuel Castells, *The Rise of the Network Society* (Oxford: Blackwell, 1996); Michael Best, *The New Competitive Advantage: the Renewal of American Industry* (Oxford: Oxford University Press, 2001).

39. Jeffery Henderson *et al.*, 'Global Production Networks and the Analysis of Economic Development', Global Production Networks Working Paper 1, 2002 available at http://www.art.man.ac.uk/Geog/gpn/wp.html.

40. Michael Best, *The New Competitive Advantage: The Renewal of American Industry* (Oxford: Oxford University Press, 2001)

41. Mario Amendola and Jean-Luc Gaffard, *The Innovative Choice* (New York: Basil Blackwell, 1988).

42. Best, *The New Competitive Advantage*.

43. Bengt-Ake Lundvall, 'The Social Dimension of the Learning Economy', Danish Research Unit for Industrial Dynamics (DRUID) Working Paper, 96–1, 1996 available at http://www.druid.dk.

44. AnnaLee Saxenian and Jinn-yuh Hsu, 'The Silicon Valley-Hsinchu Connection: Technical Communities and Industrial Upgrading', *Industrial and Corporate Change*, Vol. 10, No. 4 (2001), pp. 893–920; Hsu and Saxenian, 'The Limits of *Guanxi* Capitalism'.

45. Alice Amsden, *The Rise of the Rest: Challenges to the West from Late -industrialization Economies* (Oxford: Oxford University Press, 2001).

46. For example, see Mike Hobday, 'The Electronics Industries of the Asia-Pacific: Exploiting International Production Networks for Economic Development', *Asian-Pacific Economic Literature*, Vol. 15 (2001), pp. 13–29.

47. AnnaLee Saxenian, 'Silicon Valley's New Immigrant High-Growth Entrepreneurs', *Economic Development Quarterly*, Vol. 16, No. 1 (2002), pp. 20–31.

48. Alejandro Portes, 'Global villagers: the rise of transnational communities', *The American Prospect*, March-April 1996, pp. 74–7.

49. Etienne Wenger, *Communities of Practice: Learning, Meaning, and Identity* (Cambridge: Cambridge University Press, 1998).

50. Chen Xiangming 'Both Glue and Lubricant: Transnational Ethnic Social Capital as a Source of Asia-Pacific Subregionalism', *Policy Sciences*, Vol. 33 (2000), pp. 269–87.

51. Cf. Se-Hwa Wu, 'Dynamic production networks in the IC industry', in Ly-Yun Chang, *Corporate Networks in Taiwan* (Taipei: Yuan Liou Press, 1999) (in Chinese).

52. Walter Powell 'Trust-based forms of governance', in R. Kramer and T. Tyler, *Trust in Organizations* (Thousand Oaks, CA: Sage Publications, 1996).

53. As well noted by Saxenian in 'Silicon Valley's New Immigrant High-Growth Entrepreneurs', the overseas Indians have a software business connection with their motherland, despite being less entrepreneurial than their Taiwanese counterparts.

54. The production value of Taiwan's PC sector reached 3,380 billion US dollars in 1998, and over 29 percent of the value was created by Taiwanese investors in China (see, *Wall Street Journal*, Oct. 21, 1998). In addition, the ratio of made-in-Taiwan PC products declined from 72 percent in 1995 to 52.7 percent in 1999, and the proportion of made-in-China PC products rose from 14 percent to 33.2 percent at the same period (see Market Intelligence Center of the Institute of Information Industry. *The Year Book of Computer Industry*, (Taipei: MIC, 2001)).

55. The estimated cost savings (including material cost, direct labor and indirect labor) to Taiwanese PC companies ranged from 22 percent in mice production, to 8 percent in monitor making, in comparison with offshore manufacturing in China in 1993. The range was between 16 percent and 4 percent, in comparison with Malaysia. See Chung Ching, 'Division of labor across the Taiwan Strait: Macro overview and analysis of the electronics industry', in B. Naughton, *The China Circle* (Washington DC: Brookings Institution Press, 1997), pp. 164–209.

56. For example, the Sky Hawk Computer Group established a new company to take charge of its business with the local key customers, such as the Legend Computer and Haier Group.

57. Even though China promised to open its market to foreign companies as part of the conditions for WTO membership, there still existed many barriers, including preferential procurement policies for local companies by the governments, the existence of so-called 'dukedom' economies providing local protectionism in each province and county, and unreasonably high transportation costs and fees for non-local companies (see *Common Wealth*, Oct. 2001).

58. *China Times*, Jan. 9, 2002.

59. *China Times*, Jan. 29, 2002.

60. Su-Yu Zhuang, *Taiwanese High Technology Firms Cluster in YRD* (Taipei: Global View Publisher, 2001) (in Chinese).

61. Interview with Mr Huang P., Vice President, Inventec Group (Shanghai), Aug. 16, 2001.

62. Tse-kang Leng, 'Economic Globalization and IT Talent Flows Across the Taiwan Strait: The Taipei/Shanghai/Silicon Valley Triangle', *Asian Survey*, Vol. 42, No. 2. (2002), pp. 230–50.

63. Hsing, *Making Capitalism in China*.

64. *Electronic Engineering Times*, Jan. 14, 2002.

65. Susan Walcott, 'Chinese Industrial and Science Parks: Bridging the Gap', *The Professional Geographers*, Vol. 54, No. 3 (2002), pp. 349–64.

66. *Far East Economic Review*, June 15, 2000.

67. *Electronic Engineering Times*, Jan. 14, 2002.

68. AnnaLee Saxenian, 'Brain Circulation and Chinese Chipmakers: The Silicon Valley-Hsinchu-Shanghai Triangle', unfinished manuscript, available from the author, (2003).

69. A number of famous examples include Ta-lin Hsu of HQ, Lin of Trident Semiconductor, Lip-Bu Tan of The Walden International Investment Group, and Ken Tai of InveStar. See Saxenian and Hsu, 'The Silicon Valley-Hsinchu Connection', for the details of their contribution to the Silicon Valley-Taiwan connection.

70. Saxenian, 'Brain circulation and Chinese chipmakers'; Tse-kang Leng, 'Economic Globalization and IT Talent Flows Across the Taiwan Strait'.

71. Lundvall 'The Social Dimension of the Learning Economy'.

China's WTO Implementation in Comparative Perspective: Lessons from the Literatures on Trade Policy and Regulation

MARGARET MERIWETHER PEARSON

The debate surrounding China's ability to meet the requirements of the WTO accession package ('compliance') has tended to focus on two levels: whether the Chinese government's commitment is genuine, or whether leaders responsible for the accession package can enforce their WTO commitments by potentially recalcitrant economic ministries and local officials – especially in the face of social and economic dislocations caused, in part, by WTO-related adjustments. While discussion of compliance has been important, there are deeper issues raised by the academic literature on comparative and international political economy that cast a different light on the nature of Chinese accession. The purpose of this article is to examine some key ideas from the broader political economy literature that can help frame our understanding of the relationship between WTO as a globalizing force and the domestic politics of China's trade policy. Two parts of the political economy literature – international trade policy and regulatory policy – offer much for us to consider. This article attempts to take a modest step in this direction.

Margaret Meriwether Pearson is Professor of Government and Politics at the University of Maryland, College Park, USA.

The first of these two literatures – on international trade policy – takes an 'outside looking in' perspective. Specifically, this literature sets forth crucial assumptions about the nature of a country's behavior in the WTO, and about the behavioral expectations inherent in WTO as a trade liberalization mechanism. The literature is useful in its suggestion that much about China's compliance situation is *not* unique and, indeed, is accounted for in the WTO. The second literature addressed in this essay concerns the nature of the regulatory state in advanced industrial economies. Here, the core interest is in both the extent to which 'liberalizing' states regulate and the institutions and means by which they do so. In contrast to the trade policy literature, the comparative political economy literature draws our attention to the *internal* regulatory structures that mediate trade liberalization. The comparative scholarship on regulatory states suggests that there are wide variations in how industrial economies actually liberalize their economies – the institutional structures, ideologies, and policy instruments used.

Neither of these two literatures has been written with China explicitly in mind, and initially the two bodies of thought may appear to be too disparate to be linked in the same article. (Unfortunately, moreover, each is too broad to be given comprehensive treatment here.) But the implications of both literatures for how we should assess China's WTO accession are striking and consistent. Taken together, the literatures suggest that while the impact of the WTO on China may be deeper and more rapid than in the case of other earlier liberalizers, the issues involved and China's reactions are not *sui generis*. Moreover, these literatures argue against a notion, popular in US business circles, that the WTO dictates convergence to a single end – institutionally or regulatorily speaking – or that other countries have indeed converged to a narrow norm in terms of regulatory structures.[1]

This article is divided into three sections. The first examines the evolution of trade policy and its implications for national sovereignty in light of the broad trade policy literature. The second section examines ideas arising from the literature on regulation and the regulatory state. The final section goes on to examine the ways in which our perspective on China's implementation of its WTO agreements may be illuminated by these broader literatures, with a particular focus on the emergence of China's regulatory state in the WTO context.

FROM THE OUTSIDE LOOKING IN: THE WTO'S EXPECTATIONS FOR SOVEREIGN STATES

To read carefully about international trade policy, and the domestic politics of trade, is to understand that the situation posed by China's WTO implementation is consistent with much that we know from other countries' entrance into trade agreements. The purpose of this section is to adjust our perspective on China's WTO accession – to see that China is in important ways not exceptional – by looking at some of the established truisms about the political economy of international trade. Although the discussion is very basic, much of this perspective gets lost in analysis concerning China.

When thinking about the scholarship on the political economy of trade and the relationship of trade policy to sovereign states, two points stand out. First, the WTO as an institution is the predominant international mechanism for economic liberalization in individual nation states, second only to markets themselves. By its very nature the WTO attempts not merely to regulate trade at the borders of nations, as the General Agreement on Tariffs and Trade (GATT) in its original incarnation was designed to do. Rather, the WTO explicitly attempts to reach inside these borders to encourage a restructuring of the economic, administrative, and judicial institutions in support of trade and investment liberalization. The WTO's dispute resolution mechanism (DRM) as well as its notification, review and transparency norms attempt to establish a supra-national channel for oversight and enforcement beyond what international market forces provide. The trade theorist Jagdish Bhagwati recognized over a decade ago, as reform of the GATT was being debated, that to try to control 'inside the border' impediments to trade would be to open a 'Pandora's Box', so that the countless other barriers to trade that exist within a country would be revealed.[2] It is no surprise that, as trade agreements reach ever deeper inside borders, more problems in compliance are encountered, and the domestic politics of trade become ever more crucial for implementation.

A second generalization about the nature of the WTO's relationship with the sovereign state is that it greatly constrains the ability of the state to manage its domestic politics in relation to trade. All countries, including the US, face constraints on sovereignty from international trade agreements; the WTO, by reaching beyond borders, has taken this constraint to new depths.[3] The net benefits of these constraints are routinely debated in domestic politics, of course. Recollection of the US domestic debate over the Uruguay Round of GATT reminds us that there was substantial opposition to a WTO that would undermine the ability of government officials to manage their own economy.[4]

As part and parcel of efforts to make certain 'discriminatory' trade practices WTO-illegal, the WTO greatly weakened mechanisms available to sovereign states to manage domestic political conflict over trade. Under GATT, side-payments by governments to discontented groups served as a safety valve to siphon off discontent while the state adhered more broadly to liberal trade norms.[5] Requests by the US government to the Japanese government for Voluntary Export Restrictions (VERs) often served this function in the 1980s and 1990s. WTO rules substantially restrict the ability of governments to manage domestic groups this way, as VERs and other such arrangements have been made illegal. The prime protective mechanisms that remain legal are anti-dumping (AD), safeguards, and countervailing duties (CVDs).[6] Such remaining tools can be powerful. Moreover, the Sino-US bilateral agreement that is the foundation for China's WTO accession package incorporates very low hurdles for initiating AD, CVD, and safeguard actions against China.[7] Perhaps these tools of domestic market protection will be constrained, or even made illegal in future WTO rounds, but they have not been yet.

It is, therefore, true that the WTO puts heavy requirements for liberalization on countries, reaches deep inside their borders to do so, and removes some tools states have in the past had available to them to manage the domestic political fallout of trade agreements. These ideas would seem to support what might be called the 'globalization as convergence' or 'globalization as homogenization' literature.[8] But two *further* conclusions that might seem to grow from these homogenizing features of the WTO do *not* in fact follow, and in fact suggest the continued salience of heterogeneity in trade policy. First, domestic politics of trade have not diminished, even though some of the most common previous methods for assuaging losers are now illegal. Domestic debates over free trade agreements continue to take on a similar character: even when nations gain from trade in the aggregate, the benefits and costs are unevenly distributed, and those who are hurt tend to be more well-organized and vocal than those who stand to benefit. [9]It is often up to top governmental leaders – who may be more sheltered from such interests – to promote a trade liberalization agenda.[10] Yet even when top leaders are the most important advocates of trade agreements, and publicly articulate adherence to free trade, they look for ways to manage and even protect markets when domestic politics dictate.[11] Domestic politics – parties in control, their domestic constituencies, and national development goals – will dictate different outcomes from country to country. Although the WTO makes it more difficult to manage national politics, then, domestic politics will continue to dominate how states manage their international trade commitments.[12]

If the first conclusion that domestic politics still matters is obvious, a second conclusion is not: even as the WTO reaches inside borders, it does not create – or attempt to enforce – a *uniform* outcome in terms of institutional structure and regulatory policy; rather, the WTO, much like the European Union, embraces the possibility that the precise institutions used will vary across countries. Moreover, tools (in addition to the aforementioned anti-dumping, etc.) are amply available, notably use of standards and other prudential requirements, to prevent unfettered market access. One substantive example that is at the core of WTO principles is 'national treatment'. National treatment dictates that within a given country foreign firms are treated on equal footing with domestic firms. But rules for foreign firms must allow them to be competitive with national firms, not that they are to be treated precisely the same. Whether different sets of rules allow for 'fair competition' will be subject to much political wrangling.[13] Another example centers on 'prudential' exceptions – the notion core to WTO agreements that countries are able to establish prudential guidelines for financial institutions, so that countries can protect their financial stability. A third example concerns use of phytosanitary requirements to restrict goods for health reasons. The WTO requires all such restrictions to be based on 'sound science'. But different countries can have different science, and different credible studies can come to different conclusions. In such cases, the defending nation's science is likely to be upheld. (All three of these examples are pertinent to China's ongoing compliance process.) The notion found in the international trade policy literature that there are 'wide bands' of acceptable rules, institutional arrangements, and behavior requires a more flexible set of assumptions about what constitutes compliance than is often applied by businesses with concrete interests to defend (not to mention the governments that represent them).[14]

The WTO therefore constrains to an unprecedented degree the behavior of member states, but still leaves substantial leeway to those states as to exactly how to regulate their interaction. This latter fact suggests the great importance of examining the institutional mechanisms for regulating the economy and the great diversity among states in how they achieve this regulation. The literature on the regulatory state is addressed in the next section.

FROM THE INSIDE LOOKING OUT: WHAT COMPARATIVE POLITICAL ECONOMY TELLS US ABOUT THE REGULATORY STATE

Some writers on globalization – writers who have been very influential in shaping popular perception – have suggested that globalization forces the deregulation of trade and reduces the relevance of national borders. In other words, globalization is equated with a 'receding state' and minimalist regulatory institutions; liberalization and governmental institutions are considered to exist in a zero-sum relationship. Such views are common to supporters and critics of globalization alike.[15] But has this actually been the impact of globalization and trade liberalization on the state?

Certainly the Chinese state as it has moved to a market economy has vowed to jettison much of its managerial authority. It would be naive to argue that the 'receding state' view has no merit. At the same time, no serious student of Chinese political economy would argue that the state has receded to the level of the US state (which is itself enormous). Yet although scholars of China would criticize the notion that economic liberalization has left an anemic state, too few studies look seriously at what is *left* of the Chinese state, or at the important role that it *does* continue to play – and (the focus here) how it is, in important ways, evolving into a regulator as opposed to owner. In other words, not enough attention has been focused by foreign scholars on the emergence of a Chinese regulatory state. This section attempts to lay the groundwork for such a comparative political economy approach to the question of economic regulation. It uses the comparative literature on regulation to lay out two contrasting models of state intervention in the capitalist economy – the Anglo-American model and the developmental state model.

What is the purpose of economic regulation, that is, the rules and regulations that govern entry, exit, investment, pricing, and other functions basic to a market economy? To answer this question, the literature on regulatory states takes as its starting point the rise of the American state in the 1920s and 1930s as a regulator of market failure and protector of the health and safety of citizens. In the Anglo-American tradition the purpose of regulation is to provide the framework of rules to 'keep markets operating smoothly and as a response to the problems of market failure'.[16] The basis for economic regulation is to enforce antitrust and competition policies. Thus, the core idea is the rolling back of state authority, in favor of the market – again, the receding state.[17] This tradition also assumes an arms-length relationship between regulators and the regulated – the notion of an 'independent' regulator. Government is, in theory, detached from industry (notably banks who might otherwise preferentially allocate funds).[18] In reality, regulatory efforts are beset by the problem of asymmetric information, whereby the government regulator depends on the private sector's information to be an effective rule-maker and enforcer. Ideally, though, the state's role in promoting the nation's economic health and prosperity should be effective macroeconomic management. In developing economies undergoing privatization, added to this set of goals is the prevention of the abuse of market power by new private owners.[19]

Nevertheless, despite considerable market power, the state has a prominent role in the Anglo-American tradition. Creation of a legal structure that protects property rights is key.[20] But bureaucratic regulatory institutions also are central. There is a need to develop strong regulatory mechanisms, and strong institutions to enforce these mechanisms, so that governments can formalize and institutionalize their commitments to protecting consumers and investors – without the choking of producers' initiative. Regulatory transparency and autonomy (to avoid 'capture' problems noted above) are seen as crucial.[21] Although liberalization and use of markets genuinely mean a reduced role for the state when compared to a direct ownership role, this reduced role does not mean, even in the most liberal economies, that the state gives up its role, just that the function has shifted. Dani Rodrik and others have made clear that open economies often have big governments.[22] Thus, the regulatory state is a crucial and defining aspect of the modern state in an industrialized society, even in a globalizing world and even in an outlier-nation such as the US. This is not to say that the institutions of the regulatory state are always efficient, but they are pervasive and legitimate. It is crucial that they have authority and capacity to be effective. This observation – in essence that modern industrial economies are run by regulatory states – helps clarify the importance of understanding the rise of China's regulatory state that is responsible for administering in detail China's accession to the WTO.

The crux of the regulatory state argument, as it relates to China's WTO accession, is that, partial privatization of business and decentralization of economic activities (including trade) away from governmental control does not mean that government is out of the picture. No vacuum is created. Even if the state were to extract itself totally from ownership and management, it would retain a huge function; it must take on the role of regulator. As such, liberalization has meant, not the end of state control of the economy, but a reorganization governmental control. Liberalization has actively required the reformulation of old rules and the creation of new ones. Even the strong vogue towards competition policy, which has as its central goal the international spread of antitrust and other pro-competitive rules, envisions a central role for governmental regulation. And even in the most 'free market' economies, the establishment and protection of markets has been substantially state-driven. Private interests have made their voices felt, of course. But the state has been a (if not *the*) primary actor shaping the nature of regulation.

The contending model to the Anglo-American version of the regulatory state is that of the 'developmental state.' This literature has been most thoroughly developed with reference to Japan, but also is commonly applied to Taiwan and South Korea.[23] Japan's regulatory system, rather than being focused on competition, embraces an ideology that has developmental state roots (or 'late developer' roots, in the language suggested by Gerschenkron), using

> economic regulation to actively foster technological development, capacity growth, and competitiveness of targeted industries considered essential to the future viability of the Japanese economy. The industrial policies ... are oriented toward boosting industrial development. Security concerns have also weighed heavily in the developmentalist state agenda, ...including the fostering of the development of dual use (military and civilian) technology, embedding military production in the commercial economy, and the nurturance of domestic industries.[24]

Growing out of a developmental state model, and in stark contrast to the Anglo-American version, regulatory policy in this environment embodies deep suspicion of competition, particularly from foreign business. Rather, economic regulation in Japan is used to sustain the viability of small producers, in large part because they have provided an important electoral base for the Japanese regime. Finally, the Japanese regulatory structure tends to lack transparency and operates to a significant extent by informal rules.[25] These features lead to the conclusion that regulation, in its formal and informal dimensions, serves to retain strong bureaucratic authority (even if not coupled with state ownership) in the context of a desire to preserve large numbers of uncompetitive firms.[26]

By considering the distinction between the Anglo-American and developmentalist models of the regulatory state we reinforce the notion that the institutions and norms of regulation vary substantially from state to state. This conclusion is broadly in tension with globalist assumptions of convergence, and even with the Anglo-American roots of much of the regulatory reform literature. Yet both models serve the function of management of the economy and mediate state-business relations. They therefore are usefully brought under the same rubric, albeit at opposite ends of the spectrum.

What can we glean for China (and its WTO accession) from this literature on the regulatory and developmental states? I wish to highlight three points. First, the growth of a regulatory state is a fact of life in advanced industrial market-oriented economies. Second, contrary to convergence theories (and in some tension with the goals of the WTO), there is considerable variance in the specific regulatory institutions of advanced industrial economies, and the goals behind them. Determining the specific origins of a regulatory state is no simple matter. Suffice it to say that, in general, it is shaped by the same panoply of variables usually pointed to when discussing the origins of institutions: prior institutions, orientations (which often vary by sector), and organizational structures – particularly the autonomy of various ministries/departments and their institutional capacities.[27] The particular relationship between business and the state is also an important shaping variable, and a factor that in China is undergoing transformation.

Third, as China begins to build a regulatory state, another factor is crucial – the pressure of international economic regimes. This factor is not something that has been deeply considered by the existing literature on comparative regulation,[28] but it cannot be ignored for China. Differences in national institutions are assumed across very different trade policies and, as argued previously, are recognized by the WTO. Yet how pressures for compliance play out in the context of different national institutions, especially when these institutions are evolving, will be crucial for China. This story of course will not unfold for one or two decades (or more), but there is value in flagging the issue for observation at the present juncture.

Thus, as we try to explain the nature of China's implementation of the WTO agreement, we would be remiss not to look at the nature of the state – specifically the emergent regulatory state, the norms and history that shape it (of which socialism is a part). In other words, we cannot understand the parameters of China's application of the WTO agreement without understanding the construction of a regulatory state as a key factor in the equation. The next section of the article attempts to lay the groundwork for understanding the ongoing emergence of China's regulatory state.

CHINA'S EMERGING REGULATORY STATE

As noted at the very beginning of this article, discussions of Chinese implementation of its WTO accession agreement often raise the importance of domestic PRC institutions. But they fail to focus on the pertinent prior questions that have been so closely scrutinized in the cases of the US, Britain, continental Europe, and Japan: what *is* the regulatory structure and how are its interests shaped? Part of the problem is that the regulatory dynamic in China occurs within a black box, relatively impenetrable to analysts on the outside. But, as transparency actually grows, in large part at the impetus of WTO but also with the establishment of an administrative law regime, such questions can begin to be answered.

China's regulatory state is only now in the process of becoming institutionalized.[29] Yet even at this relatively early stage, there are signs that the development of China's regulatory state is taking its own direction. In contrast to both the Anglo-American and developmental models, the Chinese regulatory state with growing responsibility for administering an increasingly market-driven economy is emerging out of a system of a nearly totally state-owned, state-managed, and planned economy. These facts alone would seem to dictate a unique path, despite the fact that the WTO's dominant members wish to encourage a regulatory structure along the lines of the Anglo-American model rather than the developmental model.[30] The Chinese desire to build a regulatory state is by no means driven purely by WTO accession, however. The government on its own initiative has taken significant steps to build consumer-protective mechanisms as well as certain pro-competitive mechanisms consistent with the Anglo-American model, though without stellar enforcement success. Unlike the developmental model, moreover, China has been quite open to foreign investment.[31] But there are clearly developmental impulses, and these have roots in both China's state-owned governmental structure as well as in protectionism.

This section has modest goals – it tries to set some broad parameters for our understanding the rise of the regulatory state in China, and to offer some implications for how we should further study WTO accession. It is organized around three parameters for defining regulatory structures: organizational structure, bureaucratic autonomy and bureaucratic capacity, and regulatory orientation.[32] The precise shape of Chinese regulatory institutions inevitably will vary from sector to sector (banking versus automobiles versus telecommunications versus agriculture). It is these differences that will need to be mapped in detail in future research.

Organization of the Bureaucracy

Steven Vogel in his work on comparative regulation describes two modes of organization, fragmented versus centralized.[33] Britain has a fragmented bureaucracy, meaning decentralized and relatively vulnerable to influence from political leadership and private groups. Japan's is centralized, with the Ministry of International Trade and Industry (MITI) playing the dominant role. Post-1949 Chinese bureaucracy is less centralized than Japan's, and perhaps is as fragmented as Britain's.

There have been many instances of administrative restructuring in post-1949 China, yet until the reform era such restructurings were not aimed at enhancing market liberalization. During the early post-Mao reform period, the core goal of bureaucratic restructuring has been decentralization of government decision-making authority. Sometimes this took the form of deregulation as well. One of the earliest instances of deregulation was related to trade and involved the break-up of the monopoly of China's 12 Foreign Trade Corporations (FTCs) that existed at the initiation of reforms in 1978. Progressively over the course of the 1980s and 1990s, the number of FTCs was expanded, including at the local level, numbering 35,000 by 2001.[34] A large number of sectors were decentralized and deregulated in the mid-1980s, including harbors/shipping, universities, etc.[35] These moves further served to fragment bureaucratic control, and though aimed to give greater leeway to market forces, they did not rationalize the state's regulatory function. Related attempts to redefine the relationship between enterprises and government were made, in the early 1980s, under the broad rubric of promoting enterprise autonomy. (Hence the use of the slogan 'break apart government and enterprises' (*zheng-qi fenkai*))[36]. There have also been numerous efforts to streamline the bureaucracy; indeed, this was a central part of Deng Xiaoping's political reform program during the 1980s and early 1990s. Yet the mere fact of multiple waves of 'rationalization' in itself suggests they were relatively ineffectual.

In contrast to these earlier weak efforts at regulatory restructuring, the March 1998 restructuring of the State Council bureaucracy (usually attributed to the then-incoming Premier, Zhu Rongji) was a pointed effort to restructure the State Council system bureaucracy. The direct goals were to rationalize and streamline the bureaucracy, and reportedly had the intention of breaking stalemates on key issues such as enterprise reform.[37] But the institutional structure created is part and parcel of the emergence of the regulatory state. The restructuring involved cutting the number of central government ministries from 40 to 29, and trimming staff in the central government and provincial governments by half.[38] The *industrial* ministries, the core of the planning system, were a particular target. Some, such as the ministries of machine building and internal trade, were downgraded to state bureaus under the State Economic and Trade Commission (SETC), and then later absorbed into SETC at the end of 2000. The Ministry of Finance and People's Banks of China remain powerhouses in macroeconomic management, as does (though to a lesser extent) the Ministry of Commerce in the area of trade. The Ministry of Information Industry (MII) – a merger of the Ministry of Posts and Telecommunications and the Ministry of Electronics Industry, with the absorption of some electronic media and aerospace functions – provided the major exception of an industrial ministry that remained outside the scope of the SETC. Regulation of telecommunications is thus positioned to evolve with different structures and norms.

Other sector-specific ministries were reorganized, including science and technology, personnel, national defense industries, education, and labor. Still other agencies – environment, intellectual property and quality – were upgraded to vice-ministerial status. There is a central-local dimension to the 'rationaliz-ing' restructuring as well, as a system of vertical integration (placing offices under direct managerial control of their superior bureaucratic organs rather than local governments) received much attention in 1998–99 in many regulatory systems (such as quality control and safety).

The 1998 restructuring was much more far-reaching than earlier attempts. Moreover, as discussed below, there has been some effort in terms of bureaucratic ideology to make them more pro-competition and pro-consumer. This reorganization has had a major positive impact on the creation of a regulatory state that was not fully anticipated by outsiders at the time. But the thoroughness and direction of state transformation depends much on the next two dimensions.

Autonomy from Political Influence and Bureaucratic Capacity

China's bureaucracy is vulnerable to political influence, not so much from society but from other sectors within the government. This contrasts with Japan's bureaucracy, which has a high degree of autonomy. China's bureau-cracy may have more in common with the moderate degree of autonomy that characterizes Britain's bureaucracy.[39] This lack of autonomy, as well as fragmentation in structure, is captured in the dominant Western explanation of bureaucratic politics in China, 'fragmented authoritarianism', which posits that policy-making is largely a function of bureaucratic bargaining and consensus building. Several recent studies have shown a pluralization of actors in foreign-

policy making in China, including in the foreign economic policy bureaucracy.[40] But pluralization of actors may not translate into autonomy of
regulatory institutions; indeed, it may mean that there is simply more
bargaining to be done. Another complicated matter is the relationship between
a regulator and the businesses it regulates when those businesses are state-
owned is also highly pertinent. An illustrative example here is MII, which lost
ownership rights to key telecom businesses to other government ministries (the
Ministry of Finance became the 100 percent owner of China Telecom). Can it
truly be the case that the Ministry of Finance allows MII total autonomy in
regulation, especially when both have influence on the State Council, not to
mention the Politburo? Issues such as these abound in China's nascent
regulatory environment.

Bureaucratic capacity has also been the subject of reforms – reforms that
clearly influence the type of regulatory state that is emerging. The Working
Party on China's Accession to the WTO has flagged this subject as a crucial
variable in China's implementation of the agreement. As with streamlining the
bureaucratic structure, upgrading the quality of bureaucratic personnel was also
a central feature of Deng Xiaoping's reforms, and much was accomplished in
terms of raising educational standards and institutional expertise.[41] This effort to
attract the 'best and brightest' continues, particularly as it is recognized that the
oversight of sophisticated businesses in a complex technological and international environment requires great expertise.

A hugely important means for building regulatory capacity is to endow the
regulatory institutions with authority to carry out their jobs, and to define what
exactly that authority is. This task involves legal empowerment – giving legal
backing to regulatory agencies, and also the resources for monitoring and
enforcement. In this sense China can be seen as adopting a central part of the
Anglo-American model, but the success of these empowerment efforts remain
limited.

Orientation of Regulation

Distinctions between the Anglo-American and developmental models can be
made on the dimension of normative/ideational orientation. The former model
tends to foster low governmental intervention in the economy (though far from
zero, as discussed above) and a goal of efficiency via competition and
prevention of market failure. It places much value on procedures, that is,
regulators place a greater premium on administrative due process –
transparency, achieved through publication of drafts, public comment periods,
and open publication of all relevant rules – than on promotion of specific
industries. It may be noted that the WTO itself reflects this Anglo-American
model, aiming largely at promoting outcomes through the institutionalization of
principles of transparency and 'neutral' adjudication of conflicts through its
dispute resolution mechanism. The developmental model, on the other hand,
fosters a higher degree of intervention in markets, and promotion of industries
that can compete internationally, while shielding those considered socially
important even if not domestically or internationally competitive.

As with the dimensions of institutional organization, fragmentation and autonomy, the ideological story is still unfolding. Neither model is being followed fully. Rather, elements of both models are present. Some of the discourse initiated with and subsequent to the 1998 reorganization of the State Council was reminiscent of the Anglo-American model. Significant are strong pronouncements that the role of government needs to be less interventionist, as in the slogan that there should be transformation 'from a "government of permits and approvals" to a "government of regulation and monitoring"' (*you 'shenpixing zhengfu' dao 'jianguanxing zhengfu'*). These commitments have been often noted by the academic community and, increasingly, in the Chinese press.[42] Wang Yong has discussed how the 1998 reorganization left those government agencies that survived with a redefined mandate 'limited to industrial regulation and macroeconomic management rather than direct management of SOEs'. He goes on to write that 'over the past several years, a consensus has been building among leaders and the public that state monopoly must be broken, that more competition will bring a strong economy to the country and better services to consumers. Specifically, they criticize that the finance, telecommunication and distribution industries are the least reformed sectors.'[43] The development of unified (economic) law-enforcement departments as part of the 1998 reforms was done with promotion of competition in mind. Even the formation of the MII has been accompanied by the effort to create a medium of competition through the breakup of China Telecom.[44] Greater commitment to transparency and more public administrative procedures have become evident to the foreign business community moreover.[45] These latter transformations, and the related efforts to develop an administrative procedure law, are undoubtedly influenced by the WTO accession process. But the reformulation of government reaches far beyond WTO accession, and has been by no means merely instrumental for WTO approval.

At the same time, there is ample room for movement in directions reminiscent of the Japanese developmental model. In telecom, for example, MII's regulatory function is coupled explicitly with its 'planning' function, especially to promote continued penetration of telecom services to the whole of China and avoid a deepening 'digital divide'.[46] (China is far from unique in its efforts to carry out such a 'universal services obligation' in telecommunication, and indeed is being encouraged and supported in this by the World Bank.) MII, sometimes acting at the behest of the State Council, is also careful in structuring market access, not only for foreign firms but also domestic firms.

More generally, although the evidence of pro-competitive leanings are significant and need to be taken seriously, the language of competition is often coupled with a goal of promoting Chinese industries against foreign competitors.[47] Thus, for example, the State Council has encouraged some industries (notably automobiles) to consolidate themselves into 'big group' companies that can stave off foreign competition. Such plans come in the framework of continued belief that industrial policy that positions China's strategic industries (e.g. services, telecommunications, agriculture, and automobiles) is necessary.

The WTO framework leaves plenty of room to promote aspects of the developmental model. Industrial policy is not technically speaking WTO-illegal. Nor are anti-dumping measures, which China has rushed to increase in its promulgation of a largely WTO-consistent Anti-Dumping Law. Here, China appears to be following Japan's recent move into using anti-dumping as a powerful yet sanctioned protective measure.[48] Moreover, as Braithwaite notes, 'there has not been a concerted effort to harmonize competition law' within the WTO, so China (as other countries) can be expected to use whatever tools the WTO has left outside its specific commitments to promote strategic aims.[49] Furthermore, the discourse on economic nationalism remains strong, and indeed even appears to have strengthened since China's WTO accession. Such a discourse serves the interests of industries desiring protection, but it also has taken hold among many elites and citizens.[50]

CONCLUSION

This article has cut a wide swath. It has suggested that attempts to understand China's WTO implementation and, more broadly, the impact of globalization on China's political economy should include perspectives raised by the trade policy and regulatory policy literatures. The trade policy literature forces us to examine the ambiguities inherent in the institutional, regulatory, and normative foundation of the WTO that exist, even in the face of WTO's greater power (compared to GATT) and China's unprecedentedly detailed accession agreement. To understand China's implementation, distinctions must be made between outright non-compliance and divergences that are tolerated by WTO, even if poorly tolerated by business people or member governments.

The regulatory politics literature turns our attention to the mammoth task that China faces in establishing a regulatory state, especially in the time-compressed fashion that is dictated by both the domestic agenda and the WTO. The regulatory state is now taking shape, and will continue to do so for some time. As was true for the US, it is not an even process, and will be subject to myriad domestic forces. Some forces will push in the direction of an Anglo-American model, others in the direction of a Japanese developmental model. It will be influenced by WTO pressures, but not determined by them. Indeed, a key test of whether the WTO is actually a globalizing device may be how well it encourages China to avoid moving to the developmental model. The early signs are that, as is to be expected, China is moving down its own road. It is a road that is well within the parameters of existing models, but mimics none of them.

NOTES

1. As a general observation, interviews conducted in the summer and fall of 2002 with both trade lawyers (including former trade negotiators) and foreign business people indicate that the former group understood well the implications for China of the ideas presented here, whereas many more narrowly focused business practitioners were not persuaded by them.

2. Jagdish Bhagwati, 'Multilateralism at Risk, The GATT is Dead, Long Live the GATT', *The World Economy*, Vol. 13, No. 2 (June 1990), p. 155. Writing prior to the completion of the Uruguay Round, Bhagwati was concerned that this effort to reach inside borders would ultimately fail, and would leave advocates of 'managed trade' victorious.

3. See Miles Kahler, 'Trade and Domestic Differences', in Suzanne Berger and Ronald Dore, *National Diversity and Global Capitalism* (Ithaca, NY: Cornell University Press, 1996), pp. 298–332.

4. These debates are described in I.M. Destler, *American Trade Politics*, Third Edition (Washington DC: Institute for International Economics, 1995); and Anne O. Krueger, *American Trade Policy: A Tragedy in the Making* (Washington, DC: AEI Press, 1991).

5. Judith Goldstein, 'International Institutions and Domestic Politics: GATT, WTO, and the Liberalization of International Trade', in Anne O. Krueger, *The WTO as an International Organization* (Chicago, IL: University of Chicago Press, 1998), p. 151.

6. Anne O. Krueger, 'Introduction', in Krueger, *The WTO as an International Organization*, pp. 1–27 (specifically pp. 7–9).

7. Nicholas R. Lardy, *Integrating China into the Global Economy* (Washington DC: The Brookings Institution Press, 2002). As I discuss subsequently, the PRC also has recognized the utility of these tools, and has beefed up its own ability to use them.

8. Some of the most responsible examples of work which might fall into this category are found in the essays in Berger and Dore, *National Diversity*.

9. This general rule about 'vocal losers, quiet winners' has held true for China both during negotiations for the WTO in the late 1990s and immediately post-accession. An oddity, in terms of comparative politics, is the 1999 US debate on permanent normal trade relations status (PNTR) for China. There, the coalition in favor of granting China PNTR won against those who perceived they would be hurt by such a move.

10. Several studies have pointed to the crucial intervention of the top leaders in pushing through China's WTO deal. See, especially, Margaret M. Pearson, 'The Case of China's Accession to GATT/WTO', in David M. Lampton, *The Making of Chinese Foreign and Security Policy in the Era of Reform* (Stanford, CA: Stanford University Press, 2001), pp. 337–70; and Wang Yong, 'China's Stakes in WTO Accession – The Internal Decision-Making Process', paper presented at conference on 'China's WTO Accession: National and International Perspectives', Fourth ECAN Annual Conference, Berlin, Feb. 1–2, 2001.

11. See John Braithwaite and Peter Drahos, *Global Business Regulation* (Cambridge: Cambridge University Press, 2000), p. 207. The April 2002 announcement of steel tariffs by US President Bush is a prime example.

12. Goldstein, 'International Institutions and Domestic Politics'. A country's position in the world economy and its comparative advantage, in addition to creating concrete trade opportunities and difficulties, will also influence the perceptions of policy-makers.

13. The area of services is especially subject to ambiguity. For example, in the provision of legal services by foreigners, WTO member countries are allowed to set standards for how many years of practice of lawyer has before he or she is eligible to practice in another country – just as US states are each allowed to have their own standards. Whether this constitutes a barrier to market access or simply a prudent setting of standards to ensure a credible profession is subject to debate and interpretation. But the fact is that individual countries have the right to set such standards unless a WTO dispute resolution panel were to deem them as obstructing national treatment.

14. On the need for such flexibility, see Braithwaite and Drahos, *Global Business Regulation*, p. 211; and Kahler, 'Trade and Domestic Differences'. An important exception is tariff rates, where the precise outcome (result) is dictated by the agreement. But questions of national treatment and not tariff rates are the heart of domestic conflict over the WTO in most countries, including the PRC. Moreover, the bounds of what is permitted are often ambiguous and therefore subject to the kind of *political* bargaining within the WTO that is, according to Braithwaite and Drahos in *Global Business Regulation*, at the heart of the WTO reality.

15. A highly influential book that looks favorably on these political implications of globalization is Kenichi Ohmae, *The Borderless World: Power and Strategy in the Interlinked Economy* (New York: Harper Business, 1990). A critical treatment of this process is Dani Rodrik, *Has Globalization Gone Too Far?* (Washington DC: Institute for International Economics, 1997).

16. Lonny Carlile and Mark C. Tilton, 'Regulatory Reform and Developmental States', in Lonny Carlile and Mark C. Tilton, *Is Japan Really Changing Its Ways?: Regulatory Reform and the Japanese Economy* (Washington DC: Brookings Institution Press, 1998a), p. 4.

17. On the rise of the regulatory state in the US, see, March Allen Eisner, *Regulatory Politics in Transition* (Baltimore, MD: Johns Hopkins University Press, 1993); and the essays in Kenneth

Button and Dennis Swann (eds), *The Age of Regulatory Reform* (Oxford: Clarendon Press, 1989).

18. Steven K. Vogel, *Freer Markets, More Rules: Regulatory Reform in Advanced Industrial Countries* (Ithaca, NY: Cornell University Press, 1996), p. 47.

19. See Luigi Manzetti, 'Introduction: Latin American Regulatory Policies in the Post-Privatization Era', in Luigi Manzetti, *Regulatory Policy in Latin America: Post-Privatization Realities* (Miami, FL: North-South Center Press at the University of Miami, 2000), pp. 1–11.

20. On how US law promotes competition (using the tools of antitrust law, private litigation, disclosure laws, etc.) through defining private entitlements and setting preconditions for government intervention, see Peter H. Schuck, 'Law and Post-Privatization Regulatory Reform: Perspectives from the U.S. Experience', in Manzetti, *Regulatory Policy in Latin America*, pp. 24–48.

21. These elements are a crucial focus of transaction cost theory.

22. Dani Rodrik, 'Why Do More Open Economies Have Bigger Governments?' *The Journal of Political Economy*, Vol. 106, No. 5 (Oct. 1998). See also Peter Katzenstein, *Small States in World Markets* (Ithaca, NY: Cornell University Press, 1985).

23. See the recent assessment of the developmental state concept in T.J. Pempel, 'The Developmental Regime in a Changing World Economy', in Meredith Woo-Cumings, *The Developmental State* (Ithaca, NY: Cornell University Press, 1999), pp. 137–87.

24. Carlile and Tilton, *Is Japan Really Changing Its Ways?*, p. 5. See also Pempel, 'The Developmental Regime in a Changing World Economy', p. 179.

25. Carlile and Tilton, *Is Japan Really Changing Its Ways?*, pp. 7–9. For example, Japan has an Antimonopoly Law and Fair Trade Commission. The legal limits they set on bureaucratic intervention have encouraged informal intervention to circumvent them. See Lonnie E. Carlile and Mark C. Tilton, 'Is Japan Really Changing?' in Carlile and Tilton, *Is Japan Really Changing Its Ways?*, p. 199.

26. In contrast to the Chinese situation, in Japan the firms that were often being preserved were small-scale. Carlile and Tilton, 'Regulatory Reform and Developmental States', p. 198.

27. Vogel, *Freer Markets*, pp. 58–61 focuses on two variables determining the nature of *deregulation* – regime (and sectoral) orientation and organization, especially the degree of fragmentation on relative autonomy of the bureaucracy. On the rise of the regulatory state in the US, see Eisner, *Regulatory Politics in Transition*.

28. I distinguish international economic regime pressure – primarily the WTO – from the security and export pressures discussed in the developmental state models. An important exception is T.J. Pempel's analysis of 'embedded mercantilism', which depicts Japan as formally adhering to the letter of GATT/WTO agreements, but frequently undercutting these organizations through informal means. See T.J. Pempel, 'Regime Shift: Japanese Politics in a Changing World Economy', *Journal of Japanese Studies*, Vol. 23, No. 2 (1997), pp. 333–61.

29. This important topic has gone virtually unstudied or even commented on outside China. Within China there is a vigorous discussion. See, for example, the volume *Zhongguo Jichu Sheshi Chanye Zhengfu Jianguan Tizhi Gaige Ketizu* (China Infrastructure Industries Government Regulatory System Reform Task Force), *Yanjiu Baogao* (Research Report), (Beijing: *Zhongguo Caizheng Jingji Chubanshe* (China Finance and Economics Publishers), June 2002). This report contains essays written by well-known scholars Yu Hui (Chinese Academy of Social Sciences (CASS)) and Zhou Qiren (Beijing University). Two influential scholars originally from the PRC, now in US universities, have begun to bring attention to this issue. See Lu Xiaobo, 'From Players to Referees: The Changing Role of the State and Bureaucracy in China', paper prepared for the annual conference of the Association of Asian Studies, Washington, DC, April 7, 2002; and Dali L. Yang, 'Can the Chinese State Meet Its WTO Obligations? Government Reforms, Regulatory Capacity, and WTO Membership', *American Asian Review* (2002). David Zweig has raised the issue of regulatory reform in mediating the internationalization of China's economy. See David Zweig, *Internationalizing China: Domestic Interests and Global Linkages* (Ithaca, NY: Cornell University Press, 2002), pp. 264–8.

30. A key goal of the US in negotiations was to 'avoid another Japan'.

31. Lardy, *Integrating China into the Global Economy*.

32. With the exception of bureaucratic capacity, which I have added, these remaining parameters are a subset of the dimensions analyzed by Vogel, *Freer Markets*, p. 45. The business-government relationship, while ultimately crucial to any empirical understanding of the regulatory state in

China, is not considered in depth in this article. In Japan, regulatory policy tends to be dominated by 'iron triangles' or regulators, regulated firms, and politicians. See John C. Campbell, 'Bureaucratic Primary: Japanese Policy Communities in an American Perspective', *Governance*, Vol. 2, No. 1 (Jan. 1989), pp. 5–22. The rather large literature on evolving state-business relations in reform China does not parallel the 'iron triangle' literature in Japan, however, as they have been aimed at understanding evolving state-society relations and predicting political reform. Thus, the relationship between regulators and firms is a ripe area for research. Examples of work on state-business relations in China include: Bruce J. Dickson, *Red Capitalists in China: The Party, Private Entrepreneurs, and the Prospects for Political Change* (New York: Cambridge University Press, 2003); David L. Wank, 'Private Business, Bureaucracy, and Political Alliance in a Chinese City', *Australian Journal of Chinese Affairs*, No. 33 (Jan. 1995), pp. 55–71; and Jonathon Unger, '" Bridges": Private Business, the Chinese Government and the Rise of New Associations', *The China Quarterly*, No. 147 (Sept. 1996), pp. 796–819.

33. Vogel, *Freer Markets*, p. 47 and Table 5.
34. Lardy, *Integrating China into the Global Economy*, pp. 40–42.
35. See Zweig, *Internationalizing China*; and Thomas G. Moore, *China in the World Market: Chinese Industries and International Sources of Reform in the Post-Mao Era* (New York: Cambridge University Press, 2002).
36. Margaret M. Pearson, *Joint Ventures in the People's Republic of China: The Control of Foreign Direct Investment Under Socialism* (Princeton, NJ: Princeton University Press, 1991), p. 183.
37. Though not apparently a goal of Zhu Rongji's at the time, this reorganization also facilitated the ability of the central government in 1999 to offer a WTO package to the US in its bilateral negotiations that would eventually be accepted. See Wang, 'China's Stakes in WTO Accession', pp. 8–9. Wang notes (p. 9) that 'about 45% of cadres at the State Development Planning Commission had to be retired or get positions in non-government institutions including state-owned companies'.
38. This discussion is based largely on Yang, 'Can the Chinese State Meet its WTO Obligations?' The Party organization and local governments (counties, cities, towns and townships) were also downsized.
39. Vogel, *Freer Markets*, p. 47 and Table 5.
40. On fragmented authoritarianism see Kenneth Lieberthal and David M. Lampton (eds), *Bureaucracy, Politics, and Decision-Making in Post-Mao China* (Berkeley, CA: University of California Press, 1992). On pluralization, see David M. Lampton (ed.), *The Making of Chinese Foreign and Security Policy in the Era of Reform* (Stanford, CA: Stanford University Press, 2001). In the latter volume, see Margaret M. Pearson's essay, 'The Case of China's Accession to GATT/WTO', pp. 337–70, on foreign economic policy.
41. See Hong Yong Lee, *From Revolutionary Cadres to Party Technocrats in Socialist China* (Berkeley, CA: University of California Press, 1991); and Zhang Baohui, 'Institutional Aspects of Reforms and the Democratization of Communist Regimes', *Communist and Post-Communist Studies*, Vol. 26, No. 2 (June 1993), pp. 165–81.
42. An academic version of this is *Zhongguo Jichu Sheshi Chanye Zhengfu Jianguan Tizhi Gaige Ketizu*. Lu, 'From Players to Referees', p. 5, quotes the phrase from the popular magazine *Liaowang* [Outlook], No. 10, March 4, 2002.
43. Wang, 'China's Stakes in WTO Accession', p. 9 (1st quote) and p. 14 (2nd quote).
44. Kenneth J. Dewoskin, 'The WTO and the Telecommunications Sector in China', *The China Quarterly*, Vol. 167 (Sept. 2001), pp. 630–54.
45. The foreign business community has noted this widely though it wishes to see it go further. See, for example, Timothy Stratford, 'Testimony At Hearings Before The Office of the United States Trade Representative Regarding China's Implementation of its WTO Commitments', Washington DC, Sept. 18, 2002. Available at http://lists.nrb.org/japanforum/showmessage.asp?ID=5891.
46. Author interviews, Beijing, Sept. 2002.
47. The following examples are from: Wang, 'China's Stakes in WTO Accession'; Peter Nolan, *China and the Global Business Revolution* (Houndmills: Palgrave Publishers, 2001), Ch. 13; and Wu Ching, 'The Challenges Facing China's Financial Services Industry', in Nolan, *China and the Global Business Revolution*, pp. 813–38.
48. On anti-dumping and its sister strategy, countervailing duties, see Robert E. Baldwin, 'Imposing Multilateral Discipline on Administered Protection', in Krueger, *American Trade Policy*. On

Japan, see Saadia Pekkanen, 'WTO Law and Trade Politics in Japan', in Saadia M. Pekkanen and Kellee S. Tsai, *Japan and China in the World Economy*.

49. Braithwaite and Drahos, *Global Business Regulation*, p. 212.
50. Banning Garrett, 'China Faces, Debates, The Contradictions of Globalization', *Asian Survey*, Vol. 41, No. 3 (May/June 2001), pp. 409–27.

Chinese Changing Perspective on the Development of an East Asian Free Trade Area

KEVIN G. CAI

Since Deng Xiaoping initiated economic reforms in 1978, China's policy of 'opening to the outside world' has been consistently deepening and broadening, reflecting Beijing's efforts to respond actively to the changing conditions of the global and regional economy as well as the changing conditions of the Chinese domestic economy, so as to best serve the national objective of rapid economic development. In this process, two policy decisions that the Chinese government has taken over the part two decades are of particular significance, namely, the decision to join the General Agreement on Tariffs and Trade (GATT) in 1986 – the World Trade Organization (WTO) after 1995 – and the decision to form a free trade area (FTA) with the Association of Southeast Asian Nations (ASEAN) in 2001. These two important policy decisions not only reflect a sea change in the Chinese leadership's perspective on China's foreign economic relations, but they also reflect the substantive change in China's economic relations with the outside world. While these are two separate policy decisions, which were made at different times and driven by different motives under different conditions, they are no doubt logically related to each other.[1]

This article addresses Chinese changing perspective on the development of an East Asian FTA in the context of concurrent trends of globalization and regionalism in the world economy. In doing so, the study, in the first part, examines the global and regional background behind Chinese changing perspective on the issue of East Asian FTAs as discussed by Chinese scholars. The article's second section reviews the ongoing scholarly discussion and debate among Chinese academics on regional economic integration in general and regional FTAs in particular. Based on the discussion of the evolution of Chinese

Kevin G. Cai is Assistant Professor in the Department of Asia Pacific Studies at San Diego State University, USA.

thinking on FTAs in East Asia, the third section of the contribution addresses China's ongoing adjustment of policy on this issue and its recent moves to explore and negotiate FTAs with neighboring economies in the East Asian region. Finally, the article concludes with an assessment of the meaning and impact of China's ongoing moves towards the establishment of FTAs with its neighboring economies.

At the outset, related analysis requires the identification of the various forms of regional economic integration so as to have a better understanding of Chinese perspective and the current stage of Chinese policy. Under the general rubric of regional economic integration, there are not only various forms of free trade arrangements, but also other forms of institutionalized economic cooperation.

Generally speaking, there are three forms of regional free trade arrangements, namely, free trade area (FTA), customs union, and common market. These different forms of regional free trade arrangements represent increasing levels of economic integration. A FTA is a regional arrangement within which trade barriers (such as tariffs and quotas) are removed among member states. However, member states within a FTA still maintain their respective tariffs and other trade barriers against non-members. A customs union is more advanced in the degree of economic integration than a FTA. It not only involves free trade between its member states but also imposes common external tariffs on imports from non-members. A common market is the most advanced of the three forms of regional free trade arrangements in terms of the depth of economic integration. In addition to free trade among its member states and common external tariffs on non-members, a common market removes national restrictions on the movement of labor and capital among member states.

In addition to the above three forms of free trade arrangements, there is the example of the European economic union that evolved out of the previous European Community and that goes beyond free trade arrangements. Through the Single European Act and the Treaty on European Union, European regional integration has moved beyond free movement of goods, people and capital to include a monetary union, cooperation on research and technological development, and coordination on various policies (including social and regional policy, environmental policy, and even foreign and security policy) within the framework of the European Union (EU).[2]

THE BACKGROUND FOR CHINESE CHANGING PERSPECTIVE

During the Maoist period, for geopolitical and geoeconomic reasons as well as for Mao's own ideological obsession, China adopted an economic policy of self-reliance. Economic exchanges with the capitalist world were minimal, and there was no question of integrating with neighboring capitalist economies.[3] Even in the first decade of the reform era, the issue of participation in regional multilateral organizations in general and regional multilateral economic organizations in particular had been very sensitive for the Chinese government, not only because it would involve the sensitive issue of state sovereignty, but also because the Chinese still had a strong sense of isolation in the regional as well as the global community, and they tended to prefer the flexibility of bilateral as distinct from multilateral diplomacy.

Since the early 1990s, however, China, with its economy increasingly integrated into the global and regional economy following a decade of economic reform and opening, has gradually changed its perspective on the issue of institutionalized economic cooperation in East Asia. This change of attitude occurred at a time when the world economy was increasingly characterized by concurrent trends of globalization and regionalism following the end of the cold war. The first sign of China's changing attitude was illustrated by Beijing's participation in the Asia Pacific Economic Cooperation forum (APEC) in the early 1990s.[4] However, a more radical change came in the wake of the Asian financial crisis of 1997.

As many Chinese scholars explain, this sea change on the issue of institutionalized regional economic cooperation originated in the changing external conditions of the global economy and in the change in regional economic relations since the early 1990s. Particularly, like their counterparts elsewhere in East Asia, the Chinese economists and governmental officials have been showing growing concern over economic regionalism in the world economy, particularly in Western Europe and North America. According to Chinese scholars, of the three major economic centers in the world economy, East Asia is the only region that still lacks a formal mechanism for regional economic cooperation, while Western Europe and North America not only have their own established organizations but are also in the rapid process of further expansion to involve respectively the whole European continent and the whole Western hemisphere. Under such circumstances, there is consensus among Chinese scholars that unorganized East Asia is obviously at a disadvantageous position in the global competition with Western Europe and North America.[5]

Moreover, as many Chinese authors point out, there are in fact more than 140 existing regional trading arrangements in the world today, and more than 90 percent of the 144 members of WTO are affiliated with some form of regional economic institutions. As a result, more than 50 percent of world trade is now under the influence of regional trading arrangements and the growth of inter-regional trade within regional economic blocs is higher than the growth of extra-regional trade. If this process intensifies, there will be inevitably growing diversion of trade and investment flows, and the East Asian economies that remain outside any regional bloc might eventually become economically isolated, thus losing their traditional world markets, particularly in North America and Western Europe.[6]

On the other hand, Chinese scholars emphasize that over the past two decades China has established very close economic relations with neighboring economies. While China has now become the sixth largest trading nation in the world in terms of foreign trade volume, jumping from the 32nd place in 1978, 43 percent of China's trade is with East Asia. In the meantime, foreign direct investment (FDI) from East Asian economies accounts for over 60 percent of all FDI inflows in China. Obviously, the fortune of the East Asian economy will directly affect Chinese economic development.[7]

Chinese authors especially notice the increasing economic integration among China, Japan, South Korea, Taiwan and Hong Kong. According to one Chinese scholar's calculation, in the period of 1990–97, of the $1 trillion increase of exports from these economies combined, 50 percent thereof relates to exports among these five economies.[8] As there have been growing economic frictions between Western economies and East Asian economies (Japan, South Korea, Taiwan and Hong Kong in particular), the same Chinese scholar argues that the logical new outlet for these East Asian economies is the growing Chinese market, which is one of the most important reasons for deepening integration in East Asia.[9]

The Asian financial crisis particularly has brought a huge shock to China as well as to the whole region. Seeing the rapidly spreading and devastating consequences of the Asian financial crisis, the Chinese have undergone a dramatic transformation in their thinking and realized the great importance of a regional mechanism for close economic policy coordination and cooperation among the region's governments in an increasingly interdependent regional economy. Under such circumstances, there is realization among Chinese scholars of the urgent need for institutionalized regional economic cooperation so as to provide for a more stable regional economic environment.[10] As a matter of fact, it is precisely the Asian financial crisis that has directly provided the most immediate impetus for the dramatic change of Chinese perspective and policy on institutionalized regional economic cooperation in general, and regional FTAs in particular.

SCHOLARLY DISCUSSION AND DEBATE

As a result of changing international and regional conditions, there has been corresponding Chinese changing perspective on regional FTAs in East Asia. This change of Chinese perspective is reflected in the increase of scholarly discussion and debate on the issue. Involved in discussion and debate are not only many prominent scholars from such government think tanks as the Chinese Academy of Social Sciences, the China Institute of International Studies, etc., but also some government officials from the Ministry of Foreign Trade and Economic Cooperation (MFTEC) and the Ministry of Foreign Affairs.

While there are still a few Chinese authors who, concerned about the sensitive issue of sovereignty and China's multilateral obligations, remain cautious on China's involvement in a FTA in East Asia, there seems to be in general a growing enthusiasm among scholars and policy advisers for Chinese participation in more institutionalized regional economic cooperation with East Asian economies. This growing enthusiasm helped to underwrite Beijing's adjustment of policies and recent moves to explore and negotiate FTAs with its neighboring economies. Four major relevant issues emerged in related debates.

How Should Globalization and Regionalism be Assessed?

The first major issue facing Chinese scholars is how to assess globalization and regionalism in the world economy. In general, it seems that most of the Chinese scholars involved in the discussion and debate have quite positive views on the growing globalization of the world economy, which they acknowledge as an inevitable historical trend. As such, these Chinese scholars are favorable about China being involved in the process of economic globalization. On the other hand, Chinese scholars also mostly accept the argument of Western scholars of regional integration that regional free trade arrangements would help promote global free trade and economic globalization, an argument that can easily be used by Chinese scholars to provide an economic rationale for China to engage in FTAs with its neighboring economies.[11]

Moreover, many Chinese scholars also point out that participation in institutionalized regional cooperation can be used as an effective measure for nation states to fend off the negative effects of globalization.[12] Particularly, many Chinese authors argue that a regional economic grouping can help its member states strengthen their bargaining position in global multilateral negotiations and in influencing the setting of rules and regulations of the international economic system. The EU and North American Free Trade Agreement (NAFTA) are cases in point, and there is a strong reason for East Asian governments to follow suit.[13]

There is further argument that as a major economic power China should encourage economic cooperation in East Asia, which in turn would help promote and enhance China's economic development. Moreover, the strong complementarity of Japan, South Korea, China and other East Asian economies in their economic structure makes such economic relations beneficial for all.[14] As such, it is argued that China has to strengthen its economic relations with the East Asian economies.[15]

But there are a few scholars who justify East Asian integration by arguing that the global economy in the post-cold war era is actually characterized by 'regionalism' rather than 'globalization'.[16] A more radical view even goes as far as to argue that the economic integration of the EU type is the only way for East Asia to survive and prosper in the global competition, because 'globalization' is used by the US as a means to maintain its dominance in global affairs.[17]

While the majority of Chinese scholars involved in the discussion and debate are quite favorable about China's participation in regional economic integration concurrent with involvement in economic globalization, there are still a few Chinese scholars who are critical of China's orientation towards institutionalized East Asian regionalism, arguing that China's interests actually lie in 'globalization' rather than East Asian 'regionalism'. Their argument is primarily based on their analysis of China's continuing heavy dependence on the markets, capital, technology and resources beyond the region, particularly in North America, Western Europe and Oceania.[18]

Who Should Lead East Asian Integration?

A second major issue facing Chinese scholars concerns the leadership role in the process of East Asian integration. While most Chinese authors favor East Asian integration, there is discussion and debate over who should take a leading role in the process. For many Chinese authors, Japan should play a particularly important role in the process of economic cooperation in East Asia, because Japan is an economic superpower and any regional economic institution in East Asia can hardly be successful without Japan's leadership and participation. On the other hand, Japan could exert an even more important role in the global economy if a Japan-led East Asian economic grouping is formed.[19]

Some other authors emphasize the importance of Japan and China playing a joint leading role in the process of East Asian integration. According to these scholars, like the crucial role of France and Germany in European integration and the crucial role of America and Canada in the conclusion of NAFTA, the political will of the leading states, Japan and China, to cooperate and to lead regional integration is the key to the success of East Asian integration.[20]

But a few Chinese authors are quite skeptical of Japan's willingness and China's capabilities of leading East Asian integration by arguing that whereas Japan is deviating from the leadership role in the East Asian economy, China is economically not strong enough to lead. Thus, the creation of an East Asian regional grouping is still a long way off.[21]

What Form of East Asian Integration Should China Promote?

A third major issue under discussion and debate is what form of institutionalized regional arrangements China should promote and participate in. In the wake of the Asian financial crisis, some Chinese scholars suggest that China participate and take a leading role in regional monetary cooperation so as to enhance the position of the Chinese *renminbi* and promote the stability of exchange rates of regional currencies. However, the same scholars are also aware of the difficulty of monetary integration in East Asia, for as a more advanced stage of regional economic integration, monetary integration is more complicated and politically more sensitive because it involves the surrender of part of the sovereignty of member states and therefore requires high political trust among member states. Obviously, these conditions are not available yet in East Asia, given political, ideological and cultural diversities, disparities in economic structures and economic policies, lingering historical legacies, and continuing mutual suspicions.[22]

Under such circumstances, Chinese authors tend to focus on the formation of a FTA in East Asia, because as the lowest level of regional integration, such a FTA would have less sensitive political implications and would, therefore, more likely result in a successful new organization.

According to Chinese scholars, the existing regional organizations, such as APEC, ASEAN, etc., do not fully reflect the interests of East Asian economies as a whole. While in APEC, East Asian economies do not yet have a common institution that can represent their interests and speak with one voice, ASEAN, though more institutionalized in itself, is still too weak as a grouping and far from representing the whole East Asian region.[23]

As such, Chinese scholars have proposed various approaches to institutionalized economic arrangements between China and other East Asian economies. Among the major proposals, a real issue under discussion and debate is with whom China should start the negotiation and creation of a FTA. Four proposed approaches are particularly influential in this respect, namely, a Chinese FTA, a Northeast Asian FTA, a Chinese-Southeast Asian FTA, and a FTA for the whole East Asian region.

For understandable political, economic and nationalistic reasons, there are strong calls for the creation of a Chinese FTA, involving China, Taiwan, Hong Kong, and Macao. Some proposals in this category even suggest including Singapore in a Chinese FTA. According to the Chinese scholars affiliated with this group, the formation of a Chinese FTA is not only a logical result of increasingly closer economic ties and the high complementarity among the economies of the 'Greater Chinese Area', but will also benefit all the parties involved and promote the prominence and competitiveness of the Chinese economies in the world.[24] It is also argued that the WTO membership of China, Taiwan, and Hong Kong is conducive to the integration of these Chinese economies.[25] In particular, some authors argue that institutionalized cooperation between mainland China and Taiwan can help circumvent the existing political deadlock in the cross-straits relations and eventually help improve political relations between the mainland and the island and promote the political unification of China.[26]

A second group of scholars favors creating a China-ASEAN FTA first. According to these scholars, such a free trade arrangement is more likely to succeed because China and the ASEAN countries are generally equal in terms of the level of economic development. Moreover, they continue to argue, as China has a larger and more comprehensive economy than ASEAN, Beijing has more leeway in its relations with ASEAN and, therefore, is likely to steer the process of China-ASEAN integration. In response to critics who would emphasize China's competitive position vis-à-vis the ASEAN economies, those who support the China-ASEAN FTA counter that while many sectors in China and ASEAN appear to be in competition, the actual range of product specialization is more complementary than competitive. As the Chinese economy is currently still in an inferior position compared with the Japanese economy, and to a lesser extent, the South Korean economy, a China-ASEAN FTA will therefore enable China (ASEAN as well) to acquire a stronger bargaining position when negotiating a free trade pact for the whole East Asian region with Japan and South Korea in the future.[27]

Other scholars have alternatively supported the creation of a Northeast Asian FTA. The latter would start with an apparently more feasible arrangement involving China, Japan and South Korea. Their major argument is that a Northeast Asian FTA has much more potential not only because the Chinese economic structure is complementary with those of Japan and South Korea but also because a combined economic size of a Northeast Asian FTA would put

China, Japan and South Korea in a more desirable position in global competition with the EU and NAFTA. According to these scholars, although there are political, economic, ideological and historical obstacles to an institutionalized arrangement for Northeast Asia, a trilateral FTA among China, Japan and South Korea, once established, could actually bring economic and non-economic returns and create conditions that would overcome these obstacles. On the other hand, these authors argue, a China-ASEAN FTA would bring only limited returns for the development of a regional market, given the limited economic scale of ASEAN. Moreover, China and ASEAN are in competition in their respective economic structure and export structure, a fact that is not conducive to the forming of a China-ASEAN FTA. Despite this, these scholars agree that a Northeast Asian FTA could in due course expand to involve ASEAN in the future.[28]

The various scholars and policy-makers may differ on where to start but most seem to have a FTA for the whole East Asian region in mind. The question for all these authors is how China should achieve this objective – to start with a Chinese FTA and then spread to other parts of East Asia; or to start with a China-ASEAN FTA and later to expand to whole East Asia; or to start with a Northeast Asian FTA and eventually to include other East Asian economies; or, finally, to directly create an East Asian FTA without passing through any stages of sub-regional free trade development. Behind all these different approaches is the strong belief shared by all these authors that China should be in the driver's seat in the process of East Asian integration.

What Are the Difficulties and Obstacles?

While most Chinese authors are enthusiastic about the conclusion of free trade arrangements with East Asian economies, they at the same time realize the existence of difficulties and obstacles in launching any FTA in East Asia. Like their counterparts elsewhere in East Asia, Chinese scholars frequently note as the major obstacles: America's objection to a formal East Asian grouping, lack of political trust among East Asian states, lingering historical legacies left over from the prewar time, existence of territorial disputes, and existing sensitive security issues in the region, which, Chinese authors agree, will undoubtedly make the formation of a formal East Asian grouping a difficult job.[29] In particular, there is still lack of political trust between the two major powers in the region, Japan and China, whose cooperation is said to be the prequisite for any successful East Asian integration.[30]

But some more optimistic Chinese scholars believe that realizing the mutual benefits of closer economic relations, East Asian governments would be willing to move towards more institutionalized regional economic cooperation, which will in turn help improve their political relations.[31]

CHINA'S NEW POLICY INITIATIVES

Reflecting its changing perspective on the issue of regional integration, China has been increasingly active in institutionalized regional economic cooperation.

The first sign of China's changing policy was seen in Beijing's participation in APEC in the early 1990s, although APEC is not an organization of regional economic integration in the sense that is normally understood.[32] China has been very comfortable with the APEC approach to multilateral cooperation. Under this so-called 'APEC Approach', the diversity and independence of APEC members are respected, voluntary participation is emphasized, and the principle of unanimity through consultation and consensus in decision-making is accepted.[33] In 1996, China, joining hands with ASEAN, Japan and South Korea, also participated in the Asia-Europe Meetings (ASEM), a framework of economic cooperation between East Asia and the EU.

While these initial moves signaled China's emerging interest in multilateral cooperation among East Asian economies, it was in the wake of the Asian financial crisis that China began to take substantial policy actions that would lead Beijing to get involved formally in various projects of regional integration.[34]

China's first substantial move was to participate in the Chiang Mai Initiative in 2000, a regional currency swap arrangement. Under this currency swap arrangement, a bilateral currency swap and repurchase mechanism was established on the basis of the ASEAN Swap Arrangement. The swap arrangement requires that each state commit a certain amount of currency to be used whenever a partner state experiences a currency crisis and needs to borrow foreign exchanges. When an East Asian state under the arrangement faces a currency crisis, other states within the framework should come to its rescue by providing emergency aid to help ease that state's liquidity problem and prevent the spread of its currency crisis to other parts of the region. Although this is a regional mechanism based on bilateral arrangements, it was the first time that China had ever participated in a regional mechanism of cooperation. This move of the Chinese government reflects Beijing's understanding that an economic crisis in a neighboring economy, if not checked, would finally affect China itself, as the Chinese economy is now so closely interdependent with the whole East Asian economy.[35]

A further significant move for China was to participate in the ASEAN Plus Three (ASEAN Plus China, Japan and South Korea) forum (APT) and ASEAN Plus One (ASEAN Plus China, Japan and South Korea respectively) forum (APO).[36] In doing so, Beijing has accepted the notion that an economic grouping of the APT would help promote the process of multipolarity in global affairs, promote East Asian cooperation, and promote the greater role of China in East Asia and the whole Asia Pacific. As such, China has adopted the policy of 'active participation, broadening consensus, increasing mutual trust, and strengthening cooperation' to promote the formation of an APT FTA in East Asia.[37]

It is within the structure of APO between ASEAN and China that Beijing has taken by far the most dramatic move towards regional integration by concluding a free trade pact with ASEAN. This is not only a significant event in the development of regional cooperation in East Asia, but it is also an unprecedented event in China's foreign policy in general and foreign economic policy in particular.

The idea of a FTA between China and ASEAN first emerged during the third APO summit between ASEAN and China in Manila in 1999 when ASEAN was recovering from the Asian financial crisis. Realizing the vulnerability of its economy to the fluctuations in the world market, ASEAN was hoping to see China play a more important role in the regional economy and to have more cooperation with China in the regional economy. As such, Beijing proposed closer cooperation between China and the planned ASEAN FTA, a proposal that was immediately accepted by ASEAN.

In the following Singapore summit of 2000, at the initiative of China, it was agreed that an expert group be created to study the feasibility of a China-ASEAN FTA and the implications of China's WTO membership for ASEAN. After one year of research work, the expert group submitted a report to the governments of China and ASEAN countries, in which it concluded that the creation of a China-ASEAN FTA would bring a win-win situation for both sides and suggested a 10-year period for the achievement of this objective. The proposal was endorsed by both Chinese and ASEAN leaders. In the Brunei summit of November 2001, the leaders of China and ASEAN officially announced the decision, authorizing the start of negotiations at the ministerial level on the issue.[38]

According to the Framework Agreement on Comprehensive Economic Cooperation between China and ASEAN signed in 2002, ASEAN conducts negotiations with China as a unified body. The negotiation on the terms of a China-ASEAN FTA is completed by the end of June 2004 and a FTA will be established between China and the five original ASEAN members plus Brunei by January 2010 and the remaining ASEAN members will join the FTA by 2015. After the FTA is established, tariffs will be substantially lowered to 0–5 percent on all commodities (with the exception of a few special commodities) and all non-tariff barriers are removed among the FTA participating economies. At the same time, service trade and investment will also be liberalized and measures of trade and investment facilitation created within the FTA.[39] To show its 'sincerity and goodwill', China has offered to open unilaterally its market to some ASEAN members five years ahead of the opening of their markets to China.[40]

The created China-ASEAN FTA will involve a population of 1.7 billion, combined gross domestic product (GDP) of over \$2 trillion, and a total trade volume of \$1.23 trillion.[41] According to a research report of the ASEAN Secretariat, a FTA of China and ASEAN will help ASEAN increase its exports to China by 48 percent and its GDP by 0.9 percent (\$5.4 billion), while China will increase its exports to ASEAN by 55.1 percent and its GDP by 0.3 percent (\$0.9 billion). But in the short term, China's trade deficit with ASEAN will increase, given the similar economic structures between the two.[42]

A FTA between China and ASEAN is said to be only the starting-point of cooperation between the two sides. In addition to the removal of tariff and non-tariff barriers, the China-ASEAN FTA will also serve as a framework for overall economic cooperation between China and ASEAN. The whole idea is to establish a comprehensive and close relationship between China and ASEAN, involving a FTA, cooperation in finance, regional development, technological assistance, macroeconomic cooperation, and other issues of common concerns.[43]

Of various proposed approaches to institutionalized regional economic cooperation, the Chinese government finally decided to create a FTA with ASEAN first. By concluding a free trade pact with ASEAN, China obviously hopes to achieve its various policy objectives in East Asia in general and Southeast Asia in particular. Economically, a China-ASEAN FTA will help China stabilize its economic relations with ASEAN. ASEAN is China's fifth largest trading partner, while China is ASEAN's sixth largest trading partner. ASEAN is also an important source of FDI flows to China, and an important destination of growing Chinese outward FDI. More importantly for the Chinese, with growing institutionalized economic cooperation with ASEAN, Beijing will be able to develop a relationship of trust and partnership with the Southeast Asian countries, thus promoting China's foreign policy objective of developing a peaceful environment in the region.[44] In the meantime, with a China-ASEAN FTA in place, China hopes to acquire a more favorable position in the process of regional integration for the whole East Asian region.[45]

While the negotiations with ASEAN on a free trade pact were still in process, Beijing moved to sign with Hong Kong the Closer Economic Partnership Arrangement (CEPA) on June 29, 2003, following more than a year of negotiations. Under the China-Hong Kong CEPA, tariffs and non-tariff barriers on trade in both goods and services will be phased out and facilitation measures will be adopted to promote trade and investment. However, as Hong Kong already has a very liberalized trade and investment system, the China-Hong Kong CEPA is in effect designed to make China more open to Hong Kong. According to the CEPA, as of January 1, 2004, China would remove tariffs on 273 items of Hong Kong origin that are important to Hong Kong's economy, and by January 1, 2006, all tariffs on remaining goods of Hong Kong origin will have been removed.

On the trade in services, to be effective from January 1, 2004, Beijing was to implement some of the commitment it had made to WTO members ahead of schedule for Hong Kong. In the meantime, Beijing is also committed under CEPA to trade and investment facilitation by simplifying procedures in seven areas, including trade and investment promotion, customs clearance, transparency of laws and regulations, e-commerce, commodities quarantine, inspection and quality certification, cooperation among small and medium-sized enterprises and cooperation in traditional Chinese medicine development.[46] What is more important, the China-Hong Kong CEPA is seen by Beijing only as a starting-point for creating a Grand-Chinese Economic Zone, which will eventually involve Macao and Taiwan. As such, Beijing started to negotiate with Macao on a similar arrangement on June 20, 2003, just nine days before the signing of the China-Hong Kong CEPA.[47]

While moving towards FTAs with ASEAN and Hong Kong, China has also shown growing interest in more institutionalized cooperation with Japan and South Korea. At a first ever trilateral summit meeting held in Manila in November 1999, China reached an agreement with Japan and South Korea on trilateral joint research on economic cooperation among them. Under the agreement, a joint research project was formally launched in November 2000, involving three government-designated research institutes: the Development Research Center of China, the National Institute for Research Advancement of Japan, and the Korea Institute for International Economic Policy. Related joint research concluded that it is difficult to formulate a FTA among the three countries in the short run, not only because there is structural difference among the three economies but also because neither Japan nor Korea is willing to open its agricultural market. On the other hand, China is not confident enough to cooperate with much more developed economies. Despite this, the three countries still agreed in 2001 to set up a formal mechanism of economic ministerial meetings for institutionalized cooperation. They also decided to form an industrial forum to discuss the issues of common concerns.[48] Although it has not offered definite commitment yet, China adopts a fairly positive attitude to a possible FTA of China, Japan and South Korea for the future.[49]

Obviously, while the call for the creation of a FTA between China, Japan and South Korea is growing, Beijing seems to plan to start the formation of FTAs with ASEAN and Hong Kong, and then to expand them into a whole East Asian FTA.[50] No matter whether this plan will work or not, this strategy of Beijing is quite understandable from the Chinese point of view. Given the complexity of regional political and security issues, the start of institutionalized regional cooperation based on the initiatives made by smaller states in the region like ASEAN, let alone Hong Kong, rather than by a regional power like Japan is more acceptable to China.[51] By this strategy, Beijing hopes to sit in the driver's seat in the process of creation of an East Asian FTA. As such, China is active in getting involved in the APT, which, in the eyes of observers, is likely to evolve into a kind of FTA for the whole of East Asia. Moreover, Chinese Premier Zhu Rongji expressed China's view on the development of the APT at the fifth APT summit in Brunei in November 2001, that while continuing to focus on economic cooperation, the APT forum could gradually involve dialogue and cooperation on political and security issues.[52]

In addition to the moves discussed above, China has also taken initiatives with other subregions in Asia in recent years. China is promoting the process of cooperation within the Bangkok Agreement, which involves India, South Korea, Bangladesh, Sri Lanka, Laos, and China, to help the economic development of Asian developing countries. China also intends to expand the cooperation from the security to political and economic areas within the framework of the Shanghai Cooperation Organization (SCO). Besides, Beijing has participated in a joint development project of Northeast Asian countries, called the Tumen River project, that involves China, North and South Koreas, Japan, Mongolia, and Russia, and the Lanchan River-Megong River project, involving China, Burma, Laos, Thailand, Cambodia, and Vietnam.[53]

CONCLUSION

Starting with economic reforms of the late 1970s, Beijing increasingly realized that in order to develop the Chinese economy, China had to open to the outside world and to integrate into the regional and global economy. This understanding of the country's foreign economic relations led the Chinese government to open the country to the outside world. However, the key to China's opening to, and growing economic linkages with, the outside world during the first two decades of reform was the attraction of FDI into the country. FDI was, therefore, seen by the Chinese leadership as useful for China's economic development. This policy has proved effective, as it has directly contributed to China's rapid economic growth for over two decades.

China's changing perspective on the development of an East Asian FTA, together with WTO accession, in the context of concurrent globalization and regionalism in the world economy and in the wake of the Asian financial crisis can be seen as a new stage of the country's opening to the outside world in the sense that Beijing has now formally accepted the 'national treatment' principle and various other rules of the capitalist world economy as embodied in the WTO and the FTAs. This obviously represents a more advanced level of prospective integration with the regional and global economy.

In the meantime, as China has acquired increasing economic power as a result of the rapid economic growth over the previous two decades, the decision to participate in institutionalized regional economic cooperation as well as the WTO also reflects Beijing's growing confidence in overcoming the negative effects of deeper and broader integration into the global and regional economy.[54]

In a further analysis, China's active participation in institutionalized regional cooperation can also be understood as China's efforts to dispel the growing concerns and worry in the region about the economic competition and threat from an increasingly powerful Chinese economy.[55]

No doubt, China's free trade arrangements with East Asian economies, together with its WTO membership, are putting the country on an irreversible path of deepening and broadening integration with the global and regional economy.[56]

Finally, whereas Chinese changing perspective on the development of a FTA in East Asia is the result of changing conditions in the global and regional economy over the period of the 1990s, China's new policy initiatives and moves in this respect will inevitably bring significant impact on not only the political economy of East Asia but also the global political economy at large.

NOTES

The author would like to thank the Center for International Business Education and Research of San Diego State University for funding the research for this article.

1. As China has made persistent efforts for GATT/WTO membership since 1986, there now exist plenty of studies on this issue by Western scholars. However, as regional free trade arrangement is a most recent policy issue facing the Chinese government, there is still a dearth of literature on the subject in the West. For a most recent series of discussion on China and WTO, see the articles by Pieter Bottelier (pp. 397–411), Paul Thiers (pp. 413–31), Icksoo Kim (pp. 433–58), Susan D. Blum (pp. 459–72), and Godfrey Yeung (pp. 473–93), all published in *Journal of Contemporary China*, Vol. 11, No. 32 (Aug. 1, 2002).
2. For a comprehensive discussion of the EU, see David M. Wood and Birol A. Yesilada, *The Emerging European Union*, Second Edition (New York: Longman Publishers, 2002).

3. For a comprehensive study of China's foreign economic policy during Mao's period, see Lawrence C. Reardon, *The Reluctant Dragon: Crisis Cycles in Chinese Foreign Economic Policy* (Seattle, WA: University of Washington Press, 2002). Also see Shuguang Zhang, *Economic Cold War: America's Embargo against China and the Sino-Soviet Alliance, 1949–1963* (Washington, DC: Woodrow Wilson Center Press, 2001).

4. Li Xiang-yang, 'The Feasibility of Establishing a Free Trade Area among Japan, South Korea and China', *China & World Economy*, Vol. 10, No. 1 (2002), p. 13.

5. Song Deling and Li Guanghui, 'Jia qiang dong ya qu yu he zuo cu jin zhong guo jing ji fa zhan' (Economic cooperation in East Asia Region enhanced to promote economic development in China [sic]), *International Economic Cooperation*, No. 5 (2002), p. 27; Tong Fuquan, 'Bi ran de gou xiang – zhong guo-dong meng zi you mao yi qu gou xiang yu nan ti' (A Just-in-Concept: The blueprint of China-ASEAN free trade zone [sic]), *Intertrade*, No. 2 (2002), pp. 24–25.

6. Song and Li, 'Economic cooperation in East Asia Region', p. 27; Zhong Wei, 'Wu ren fu ze ya zhou' (No one is responsible for Asia), *China Reform*, No. 2 (2002), pp. 16–17.

7. Song and Li, 'Economic cooperation in East Asia Region',pp. 28 and 30.

8. Wang Jian, 'Cong 'ni ke song zhu yi' kan shi jie xin ge ju' (To look at the pattern of the new world from Nigersonism [sic]), *China Reform*, No. 2 (2002), p. 12.

9. Ibid.

10. Kevin G. Cai, 'Is a Free Trade Zone Emerging in Northeast Asia in the Wake of the Asian Financial Crisis?', *Pacific Affairs*, Vol. 74, No. 1 (Spring 2001), p. 11; Richard Stubbs, 'ASEAN Plus Three: Emerging East Asian Regionalism?', *Asian Survey*, Vol. XLII, No. 3 (May/June 2002), pp. 448–50; Song and Li, 'Economic cooperation in East Asia Region', p. 27.

11. See, for example, Fang Du, 'Jing ji quan qiu hua yu qu yu hua ying xiang qu shi ji dui ce', (Economic Globalization and Regionalization: Impact, Trends, and Strategy), *International Economic Cooperation*, No. 7 (2002), pp. 42–43; Wang Hexing, 'Jing ji quan qiu hua ji qi shi dai te zheng', (Economic Globalization and its Characteristics of the Times [sic]), *International Studies*, No. 2 (2002), pp. 12–13; Li Changjiu, 'Jing ji quan qiu hua yu shi jie xing shi' (Economic Globalization and World Situation), *International Studies*, No. 2 (2002), pp. 14–20.

12. Wang, 'Economic Globalization and its Characteristics of the Times', p. 12.

13. Li, 'The Feasibility of Establishing a Free Trade Area', p. 12.

14. Song and Li, 'Economic cooperation in East Asia Region', p. 29.

15. Ibid., p. 27.

16. See, for example, Wang, 'To look at the pattern of the new world from Nigersonism', p. 12.

17. Weng Tiejun, 'Wu fa fu zhi de xian dai hua' (Modernization can't copy), *China Reform*, No. 2 (2002), p. 15.

18. For such a view, see He Fan, 'Zhong guo zhan lue – quan qiu hua' (China's Strategy – Globalization), *China Reform*, No. 2 (2002), pp. 24–25. For a review of competing views on the issue of globalization, see Lu Zhengyang, 'Guan yu jing ji quan qiu hua wen ti' (On Economic Globalization), *China Economic & Trade Herald*, No. 7 (2002), pp. 12–14.

19. Song and Li, 'Economic cooperation in East Asia Region', p.31; Qin Haijing, 'Zhong guo de xuan ze: 10 + 1' (Chinese Choice: '10 + 1'), *China Reform*, No. 2 (2002), pp. 20–21. Wang Yizhou also expresses a similar view when discussing the issue of Asian regional union, cited from Pan Guangjun, 'Shui lai ling dao ya zhou: ri ben hai shi zhong guo' (Who does lead Asia: Japan or China? [sic]), p. 19.

20. See, for example, Qin, 'Chinese Choice: "10 + 1"', p. 21; Gao Lianfu, 'Yu ji you li geng yu ren you li – Zhong guo he ri ben yu dong men guo jia qu yu jing ji he zuo fang an bi jiao' (Positive-sum – A Comparison of the Chinese and Japanese plans for Regional Economic Cooperation with ASEAN), *Intertrade*, No. 4 (April 2002), p. 20. But a few Chinese scholars do not think it necessary to have a leadership role in a regional economic organization. The scholars with this view are obviously in a minority. See Li, 'The Feasibility of Establishing a Free Trade Area', p. 13.

21. See, for example, Zhong, 'No one is responsible for Asia', p. 17.

22. See, for example, He Li-ping, 'East Asian Monetary Cooperation: Necessities and Constraints', *China & World Economy*, Vol. 10, No. 1 (2002), pp. 15–19; Liu Shuguang, 'Dong ya huo bi he zuo de qian jing yu zhong guo de zuo yong' (Monetary Cooperation in East Asia: Prospect and China's Role), *International Economic Cooperation*, No. 2 (2002), pp. 59–62.

23. Song and Li, 'Economic cooperation in East Asia Region', pp. 27–29.

24. See, for example, Chi Fulin, '" Zhong guo zi you mao yi qu" jian cheng qi hou' ('The free trade area of China' will form step by step), *China Reform*, No. 2 (2002), pp. 22–23; Wei Yanshen,

'Ming zhi xuan ze – jian li zhong hua zi you mao yi qu chu tan' (A Wise Option: Tentative ideas on the establishment of China free trade zone [sic]), *Intertrade*, No. 5 (May 2002), pp. 29–32; Cao Xiaoheng, 'Zhong guo da lu jing ji zou xiang yu liang an jing ji he zuo qian zhan' (Mainland China's Economic Trend and Perspective of the Economic Cooperation between the Both Sides of the Taiwan Straits [sic]), *Taiwan Studies*, No. 2 (2002), pp. 15–22.

25. Yan Shenggang and Guo Can, 'Quan qiu hua bei jing xia de zhong guo ru shi: jin cheng, ji yu yu tiao zhan' (China's Entry into WTO in the Context of Globalization: Opportunities and Challenges), *International Studies*, No. 1 (2002), p. 19.

26. Zhou Zhihuai, 'Lun hai xia liang an jing mao guan xi de zhi du hua an pai' (On the Systematizing Arrangement of the Cross-Strait Economic and Trade Relations [sic]), *Taiwan Studies*, No. 2 (2002), pp. 7–14.

27. See, for example, Feng Xiao-ming, 'China and ASEAN Can Share the Prosperity Together – Interview with Zhang Yun-ling, Director, Institute of Asia-Pacific Studies, CASS', *China & World Economy*, Vol. 10, No. 1 (2002), p. 7.

28. For this view, see, for example, Li, 'The Feasibility of Establishing a Free Trade Area', pp. 9–14.

29. Zhong, 'No one is responsible for Asia', p. 17.

30. For more discussion on this issue, see Cai, 'Is a Free Trade Zone Emerging in Northeast Asia?', pp. 7–24.

31. Feng, 'China and ASEAN Can Share the Prosperity Together', p. 7.

32. Li, 'The Feasibility of Establishing a Free Trade Area', p. 13.

33. Tang Jiaxuan and Shi Guangsheng, 'Actively Participating in Regional Cooperation To Host the APEC Grand Meeting of the Century', *Renmin Ribao* (People's Daily), Oct. 16, 2001 (from 'China: Tang Jiaxuan, Shi Guangsheng on Hosting Successful APEC Meeting in Shanghai', FBIS-CHI-2001-1016, http://wnc.fedworld.gov, Oct. 16, 2001).

34. Feng, 'China and ASEAN Can Share the Prosperity Together', p. 3; Li, 'The Feasibility of Establishing a Free Trade Area', p. 9.

35. Feng, 'China and ASEAN Can Share the Prosperity Together', p. 3.

36. For a discussion of APT and APO, see Stubbs, 'ASEAN Plus Three: Emerging East Asian Regionalism?', pp. 440–455.

37. Song and Li, 'Economic cooperation in East Asia Region', p. 31.

38. Wei Min, 'Zhong guo dong men zi you mao yi qu de gou xiang yu qian jing' (The Conceptualization of China-ASEAN Free Trade Area and Its Prospect), *International Studies*, No. 4 (2002), p. 51.

39. Ibid., pp. 52–54.

40. Gao, 'Positive-sum', p. 21.

41. Wei, 'The Conceptualization of China-ASEAN Free Trade Area and Its Prospect', p. 52.

42. Cited from ibid., p. 53.

43. Feng, 'China and ASEAN Can Share the Prosperity Together', p. 7.

44. Wei, 'The Conceptualization of China-ASEAN Free Trade Area and Its Prospect', p. 53.

45. The above discussion of the China-ASEAN FTA relies heavily on Kevin G. Cai, 'The ASEAN-China Free Trade Agreement and East Asian Regional Grouping,' *Contemporary Southeast Asia*, Vol. 25, No. 3 (2003), pp. 395–400.

46. 'Wen: CEPA is special arrangement under "one country, two systems"', *China Daily*, June 29, 2003, available at: http://www1.chinadaily.com.cn.

47. 'Zhuan jia zhi nei di yu xiang gang CEPA shi "da zhong hua jing ji quan" de qi dian' (Experts Note that Mainland-Hong Kong CEPA Is the Starting Point of the 'Grand Chinese Economic Zone), *China News*, June 29, 2003, available at: http://www.chinanews.com.

48. Feng, 'China and ASEAN Can Share the Prosperity Together', p. 4.

49. Li, 'The Feasibility of Establishing a Free Trade Area', pp. 9 and 13.

50. Wei, 'The Conceptualization of China-ASEAN Free Trade Area and Its Prospect', p. 55.

51. Hu Zhaoming, 'Dong ya he zuo de xian zhuang yu wei lai' (East Asian Cooperation: Present and Prospects), *International Studies*, No. 1 (2002), p. 23.

52. Ibid., p. 25; Qin, 'Chinese Choice: "10 + 1"', p. 21. A Chinese scholar, Wang Yizhou, also expresses a similar view when discussing the issue of Asian regional union, cited from Pan, 'Who does lead Asia: Japan or China?' p. 19.

53. For a general discussion of this issue, see Song and Li, 'Economic cooperation in East Asia Region', p. 31. For a specific discussion of SCO, see Li Gang and Liu Huaqin, 'Final Target: Research on Development Model of Regional Economic Cooperation for Shanghai Cooperation Organization', *Intertrade*, No. 3 (March 2002), pp. 4–11. For a specific discussion of the Tumen

River project, see Andrew Marton, Terry McGee, and Donald G. Paterson, 'Northeast Asian Economic Cooperation and the Tumen River Area Development Project', *Pacific Affairs*, Vol. 68, No. 1 (Spring 1995), pp. 8–33.

54. Feng, 'China and ASEAN Can Share the Prosperity Together', p. 3.
55. Dong Fureng, 'On "Theory of China Threat"', *Hong Kong Ta Kung Pao*, Feb. 2, 2002 (from 'PRC Economist Refutes Theory of China as Economic Threat to Asian Countries', FBIS-CHI-2002–0202, http://wnc.fedworld.gov, Feb. 2, 2002).
56. Li, 'The Feasibility of Establishing a Free Trade Area', p. 9.

New and Old Regionalism:
The Shanghai Cooperation Organization
and Sino-Central Asian Relations

SUN ZHUANGZHI

The 'Shanghai Cooperation Organization' (SCO) developed out of the 'Shanghai Five Heads Convocation Mechanism'.[1] The latter was established when on April 26, 1996, Kazakhstan President Nazarbayev, Kyrgyzstan President Akayev, Tajikistan President Rakmonov, Russian President Yeltsin and China's President Jiang Zemin signed the five-country 'Treaty on Strengthening Trust in Military Affairs in the Border Regions'.

It is relatively easy to trace the rapid movement towards the formal establishment of the SCO, but, while the latter's important contribution to new regionalism is stressed in the following analysis, it is readily recognized that the pluses and minuses of this new organizational development are somewhat difficult to nail down. On April 24, 1997, the five state leaders of China, Russia, Kazakhstan, Kyrgyzstan and Tajikistan gathered in Moscow to sign 'The Treaty on Mutual Reduction of Military Forces on the Borders'. This treaty's signatories agreed not to resort to military force and threats and to reduce their respective border military forces to a low level commensurate only with the requirements of defense.

On July 3, 1998, China's President Jiang Zemin, Kyrgyzstan President Akayev, Kazakhstan President Narzhaerbayev, Tajikistan President Rakhmonov and Russia's Presidential Emissary met in Almaty. The foreign ministers of five

Sun Zhuangzhi is presently Director, Central Asian Department, Institute for East European, Russian and Central Asian Studies, Chinese Academy of Social Sciences, Beijing.

countries signed a joint statement, stressing the need to strengthen cooperation and consolidate regional peace and stability.

On August 24, 1999, the heads from five countries converged in Bishkek, the capital of Kyrgyzstan and stressed the role of the five countries in regional security and the need to take severe measures against all the various forms of extremism, separatism and terrorism.

At their July 5, 2000 meeting in Dushanbe, the five heads of state issued the 'Dushanbe Statement', which required the development of multi-level coopera- tion within the SCO, stressed economic and security cooperation and agreed to establish an anti-terrorism center and to attack the 'three forces', namely, extremism, separatism and terrorism.[2]

On June 14 and 15, 2001, the six heads of state from China, Russia, Kazakhstan, Kyrgyzstan, Tajikistan and Uzbekistan assembled in Shanghai and signed 'The Declaration of Shanghai Cooperation Organization' which formally established regional cooperation between their respective six nations. These six heads of state also signed the 'Shanghai Convention on Attacking Terrorism, Separatism and Extremism', as well as a joint statement accepting Uzbekistan's membership into the SCO.

The SCO declaration stressed that every member should strictly honor the principles of good neighborliness, equality and mutual benefit, friendly cooperation and common development, and should maintain steadfast non- alignment and practice and an open policy towards the outside world that resists action directed against other specific countries and regions and embraces friendly relations and cooperation with other regions and international organizations in the world. The declaration also spells out how the 'Shanghai Spirit', as it was formed in the 'Shanghai Five' process of 'Shanghai Five', embodied the basic content of 'mutual trust, mutual benefit, equality, negotiation, respect for diverse civilizations and the search for common development', and how these principles were to inform the mutual relations of the SCO member countries. The SCO Declaration took as its *raison d'etre* opposition to the 'three forces' and the need to provide the legal basis for the struggle against these forces.

On June 7, 2002, the six SCO heads of state gathered together in St Petersburg, and signed various key documents including 'The Charter for the Shanghai Cooperation Organization', 'Treaty Regarding Anti-Terrorist Organi- zation', and 'The Declaration of the Heads of the Member States of the Shanghai Cooperation Organization'. According to the SCO 'Charter', the basic purpose and task is to strengthen mutual trust and friendly neighborhood relations among the members. The latter are committed to developing cooperation in the various subregions; to maintaining and strengthening regional peace, security and stability; to the promotion of the establishment of democratic, impartial and reasonable new international political and economic order; and to join forces in any attack on all kinds of terrorism, separatism and extremism, as well as on the illegal sale of drugs, weapons, other transnational crimes and illegal migration. They are also to encourage effective regional cooperation in politics, economy and trade, national defense, the implementation of law, environmental protection, culture, science and technology, education, energy and resource, communications, financial credit and any other areas of mutual interest.

In order to implement the Charter's declared purposes and responsibilities, the organs within the SCO framework are to include: the heads of state conference, governmental heads' (premiers) conference, foreign ministers' conference, specific sector leaders' conference, the council of state coordinators, the regional anti-terrorist center and the secretariat. The secretariat is the SCO's permanent administrative organ; it is responsible for organizing technological security within the SCO framework, and it is located in Beijing.

Kazakhstan, Kyrgyzstan, and Tajikistan share borders with China. As participants in the 'Shanghai Five' process they together with China reached consensus on expanding security and economic cooperation. Similarly, in 2001, Uzbekistan participated in the Shanghai Five process in order to realize the same goals, but at the same time Uzbekistan was looking for ways of strengthening its security, trade and political cooperation with the People's Republic of China (PRC).

For the past 12 years, the bilateral relations between China and the Central Asian countries have developed to a much higher level. Politically, the leaders have often visited each other, and signed a series of statements, contracts and other cooperation documents, which provide the legal basis for the development of friendly relations. Economically, the specific cooperation between the two sides resulted in preliminary success, and trade volumes have steadily increased, reaching, in the last couple of years, $2 billion. Kazakhstan, Kyrgyzstan, and Uzbekistan are the main trade partners with China in Central Asia.

In security terms, the military diplomacy between China and the four Central Asian countries has increased in frequency, and China has provided the Central Asian countries with security protection and material assistance. Culturally, exchange between the two sides has become frequent and is expected to expand. The SCO's establishment has created new opportunities for raising to a higher level the development of the relationship between China and the Central Asian countries.

In the first place, in political terms, forward movement in the definition of the principles of mutual trust and equality and mutual participation in international affairs can consolidate bilateral cooperation and the basis for cooperation in mutual interest. Each time a treaty or contract is set up, it serves as a supplement and extension to the bilateral cooperation between China and the Central Asian countries

Secondly, in economic terms, attempts to facilitate trade and investment in economy and to implement cooperative programs in the areas of energy, communications and transportation, promote the further development of mutual economic cooperative relations between China and the Central Asian countries. What is more, multilateral cooperation will benefit the initiation of big investment cooperative programs.

Thirdly, in the terms of mutual trust and security cooperation, we can look forward to the peaceful and friendly new borders between China and the Central Asian countries and these same terms will directly contribute to the maintenance of regional stability and peace on the Euro-Asian continent. The cooperation between China and the Central Asian countries on attacking the 'three forces' and transnational crime became the key components of SCO security cooperation. The SCO's anti-terrorism center has had its headquarters in Bishkek, the capital of Kyrgyzstan.

At present, the incomplete character of the institutionalization and legalization of SCO organization, as well as some accompanying problems, have complicated relations between China and the Central Asian countries. In the specific internal organization and economic development of each country there is unevenness. All of the six countries are developing countries. Among them, China and Russia are big regional powers. Kazakhstan and Uzbekistan might be seen as middle powers at a secondary regional level. Kyrgyzstan and Tajikistan are poor and weak countries. The mutual benefits of economic cooperation among these countries are not obvious. Even if this kind of opportunity for cooperation exists, the mistrust between the states can render the cooperation meaningless. The partnership between Russia and China still needs more trust and understanding. Kazakhstan and Uzbekistan, as two Central Asian powers, are often in conflict.

On September 14–15, 2001, the SCO heads of state of the SCO members met in Almaty and signed the 'Memorandum of Regional Economic Cooperation'. Every country stressed the need to create conditions beneficial to economic cooperation among the six countries, including the need to develop communication corridors and to reduce tariff barriers. Throughout 2002 there was a sequence of meetings regarding national dependence, culture, public security, economy and trade, and many documents were signed. The latter emphasized principles of cooperation, but this, in and of, itself, was not sufficient to obviate the very real difficulties of implementation. In these circumstances, strengthening the cooperation between China and the Central Asian countries, namely using bilateral cooperation to promote multilateral cooperation will be especially important for the consolidation and development of the SCO.

THE FUTURE OF ORGANIZATION IN CENTRAL ASIA

Four of the six members of the Shanghai Cooperation Organization are Central Asian countries, and this will have a very great bearing on how cooperation will be organized. Central Asia is an inland region that joins Europe and Asia, with Russia to the north, China to the east, Afghanistan to the south-east, and Iran to the south-west. To the west it links the Caucasus region through the Caspian Sea. The region's total land area is about 4 million square kilometers. Historically, the region was the key to Euro-Asian communication by land. Although the geography and climate conditions are inhospitable and the geographical structure is complicated, the region has numerous types of metallic and non-metallic minerals as well as plenty of strategic resources. Central Asia has a population of 55 million. Many of these countries are economically underdeveloped. Kyrgyzstan and Tajikistan are in effect the lowest income states on the Euro-Asian continent. The Central Asian countries urgently need to take advantage of international cooperation to promote their own rapid development.

Nothing can substitute for the role of the SCO in transnational economic cooperation. The productive potential of this organization is truly great. The model for the foreign trade cooperation of the Central Asian countries is by and large the same: export natural resources, import technical equipment and middle- or low-level consumer goods. Their main trade partners are the Western countries. The Central Asian countries ship their natural resources mainly to Europe and their foreign investments and technology are mainly from the West.

The Chinese model, on the other hand, is different in the following way. China mainly exports labor-intensive commodities and imports technology and natural resources. China's most important trading partners are also the Western countries, and China's products are mainly exported to the Asian-Pacific region. Its foreign investments and technology are also mainly from the West. For these reasons, the trade in commodities of China and the Central Asian countries is mutually complementary. China needs natural resources and exports labor-intensive commodities; the central Asian countries, on the other hand, need labor-intensive commodities and export resources. But the mutual provision of advanced technology and investments between China and the Central Asian countries is still relatively limited.

The trade model for China's western region is closer to that of the Central Asian countries, namely, the export of natural resources and the import of the commodities. Thus, when considering the economic and trade relations between China and the Central Asian countries it is not enough just to make use of regional and bilateral advantages, instead, it will be necessary to develop a more comprehensive and wider cooperation. Within the SCO framework, China, Central Asia and Russia will develop one kind of good cooperative relationship relating to commodities, capital and technology. With the development of China's economy, the proportion of technology and capital as a percentage of total exports will be increased. The Central Asian countries will especially welcome this.

There is a close relation between Central Asian regional security and changes in the international environment. On the one hand, the change in world conditions will provide the Central Asian countries with opportunities to maintain their security and independence; generally international conditions tend to favor the stability of the Central Asian countries and multipolarity and the globalization process is influencing international security relations.

On the other hand, as developing countries, the five countries in Central Asia are facing unfavorable security conditions. Some observers would suggest that the area of the Central Asian countries is just at the point of 'splitting', or in 'the zone of fragmentation' that emerged with the sudden elimination of the bipolar structures of Cold War confrontation. There is an array of mounting contradiction in the complexities of distressed economic, ethic, cultural and social conditions. The resurgence of Islam has intensified historical animosities. The Central Asian leaders have come to realize that there are many factors that can fundamentally threaten the security and stability of the region, as well as individual states. These include regional military conflicts, the expansion of the forces of religious extremism and ethnic national extremism, transnational crime, great power chauvinism, and ecological crises.

The concept of security has moved beyond the political and military security spheres and has already expanded into the economic, social and other spheres. The Central Asian countries consider that regional security is characterized by its extensiveness, integral relations, immediacy and many points of complexity and that this all requires a new type of multilateral cooperative security mechanism.

To be sure the SCO has only been established for a short time, and its functions and its impact need development and clarification. In the predictable future, the SCO will not be able to play the dominant role in Central Asia. This is because the SCO is still not the highest priority in Central Asian foreign policy. That is to say, in the Central Asian view, the significance of the SCO is presently more symbolic, than practical.

There are a number of real problems in the foreign strategies of the Central Asian countries that could serve to harm the development of the Shanghai Cooperation Organization.

In the first place, the foreign strategies of the Central Asian countries ought to give priority to the need to maintain independence. The Central Asian countries' fear of Russia and China has dampened their enthusiasm for taking part in comprehensive cooperation. The Central Asian countries have predicated their policy for independence and sovereignty in the balance of power and the pluralization of their foreign relations.

Secondly, the foreign relations strategy of the Central Asian countries has to meet the needs of economic development, but the SCO has yet to make significant gains in the economic sphere. China and Russia are great powers that are still developing themselves, and they are unable to provide a lot of economic aid to the Central Asian countries.

Thirdly, the foreign strategies of the Central Asian countries are primarily focused on the Commonwealth of Independent States and the West. This is the premise for their participation in international cooperation. At present the influence of China is still not that powerful in Central Asia.

Fourthly, there is also variance among the foreign policies of the Central Asian countries. The aims of Kazakhstan and Uzbekistan are different from those of Kyrgyzstan and Tajikistan. Besides, the Central Asian countries lack experience in participating in multilateral cooperation. Their door was closed for a long time to the outside world. They have only been on the international stage for a short time. Their diplomacy is not yet well developed and their policy lacks stability. This means that they are easily swayed by immediate consideration of losses and gains and this complicates long-term planning.

At the same time, one ought to recognize that there are also some points in the foreign policies of the Central Asian countries that are beneficial to the development of the SCO.

Firstly, the foreign relations strategies of the Central Asian countries do emphasize comprehensive participation in international cooperation.[3] Secondly, the foreign policy-making of the Central Asian countries is deeply affected by history and culture. There have been 2,000 years of friendly contacts between China and Central Asia, and it would indeed by difficult to sever the traditional ties between Russia and Central Asia. Thirdly, the foreign strategies of central Asian countries are obviously affected by geopolitical factors. Their landlocked status makes these countries well disposed to developing relations with neighboring countries. Fourthly, security occupies a central place in the foreign strategies of the Central Asian countries. The maintenance of stable, friendly and cooperative relations with China and Russia is very important to regional security.

The post-9/11 change in the conditions of Central Asia has had a direct impact on the development of the SCO organization. The US-led initiative in the war against terror and the different stances of the Central Asian countries (for example, Uzbekistan strengthened its cooperation with the USA in security) poses new challenges to the SCO. Each member country has made corresponding adjustments in their foreign policy and security strategies and what they require from the SCO has changed to varying degrees. This will make the SCO less attractive and influential in the area of Central Asian security. Among the Central Asian countries, Uzbekistan obviously adjusted its foreign policy, drawing comprehensively towards the US and strengthening military and political cooperation with the US. On March 12, 2002, Uzbekistan and the US proclaimed the strengthening of comprehensive cooperation in 'The Declaration of Strategic Partnership and Cooperative Framework'. The Uzbekistan leaders publicly asserted that the position of the US has to be considered in the resolution of Central Asian problems, especially with regard to security problems.

The Central Asian countries *must find a balance between the Shanghai Cooperation Organization and the US.* Both the SCO and the US are important to the Central Asian countries. SCO members share common borders. It is unimaginable for the Central Asian countries to develop their economies and maintain domestic stability without support from their neighbors. After '9/11', the US has not only increased its own economic aid, but has also pressed the International Monetary Fund to increase its investments in Central Asia. In January 2002, Uzbekistan signed a basket treaty with the International Monetary Fund and got financial support for its economic reform. Kazakhstan argued that it is only fair that each member country have a voice in the SCO, so as to deal with the influence of the great powers and hence the SCO mechanism must operate on the basis of equality. The Kyrgyzstan leaders have emphasized that the US Army's access to Central Asia ought not to be construed as in opposition to the development of the SCO.

The Central Asian countries have stressed the need for future organization to adjust the areas of cooperation. Uzbekistan believes that since the current Central Asian security situation has already changed and the forces of extremism and terrorism have already experienced defeat, then cooperation in other areas, especially in those areas relating to economic cooperation, should be given more attention. The Central Asian countries argue that the SCO has a role to play in the coordination of relations among member countries and that it can help to avoid conflicts of interest in Afghanistan and Central Asia. Kazakhstan considers that the first thing that the SCO ought to do is foster the region's internal stability and to take Kazakhstan's own purported 'Measures for Asian Mutual Cooperation and Trust' as the complementary basis for SCO meetings or even as the core of SCO's 'Asian views'. Kazakhstan's aim is to enhance its international status through the organization and to avoid taking on too many responsibilities and especially to avert any confrontation with the US and other Western countries.

The Central Asian countries *consider that the SCO should place much more emphasis on the interests of small countries.* The Central Asian countries argue that China and Russia are great powers and play crucial role in the SCO organization, thus they should, even if it means sacrificing their own interests, help the middle or small countries in Central Asia to develop their economies. Uzbekistan points out that conditions in the six countries are different: that China is in a superior economic position and that while the Central Asian countries are at disadvantage in this aspect, economic cooperation cannot be started too hastily, as the Central Asian countries are experiencing difficulties in immediately opening up their markets.

The attitudes of the four Central Asian countries are not the same. Both Kazakhstan and Uzbekistan want to play an important role in the region and hope to take advantage of the SCO's prestige. On the other hand, Kyrgyzstan and Tajikistan think that participation in the SCO's cooperation will help them solve domestic issues of economy and stability. Kyrgyzstan correlates domestic stability with security cooperation within the SCO framework and thus proposed to locate the organizations' anti-terrorist center in its capital. In October 2002, it became the first to hold joint anti-terrorist military maneuvers with China.

The Central Asian countries when they are involved in cooperative activities in the region often take into account the SCO, but they are even more interested in their own country's 'interests' and 'needs'. The economic capabilities of the Central Asian countries are limited and domestic political contradictions are likely to become exacerbated, thus they are quite enthusiastic about cooperation within the organization, and they may even try to get more support and help from China and Russia by playing an ostensibly 'subordinate' role in the organization.

SEVERAL FACTORS AFFECTING THE MULTILATERAL COOPERATION BETWEEN CHINA AND THE CENTRAL ASIAN COUNTRIES

Central Asia is an important region for China. In order to maintain stability and continuous development, China needs a stable periphery. As the neighbor of China, Central Asia is one important part of China's environment. Central Asian countries provide new opportunities for China's economy, especially the north-west region of China. On the international stage, China and Central Asia share a number of common interests. China aims to become one of several poles in world politics, and the Central Asian countries are once again trying to become the bridge between the East and the West. A variety of objective factors are pushing the two sides to strengthen their cooperation.

Since independence, the five Central Asian countries have attached a great deal of importance to the development of friendship with China. In the making of their foreign policy, China occupies an exceptionally important place. This is objectively confirmed by the following:

In the first place, China is a big power, bordering Central Asia. The two sides share long borders. The borders between China and Kazakhstan, Kyrgyzstan and Tajikistan are respectively 1,700 kilometers, 1,000 kilometers and 400 kilometers. Historically, China and the Central Asian countries had very close relations. The starting-point of the 'silk road' which brought prosperity to the Central Asian region was in China.

Secondly, the five Central Asian countries are all inland countries and have no outlets to the sea. China provides them with the most convenient and reliable transportation corridor to the Pacific Ocean. Since the second Euro-Asian continental bridge opened in 1992, the Central Asian countries have had expectations regarding this. In 1996, Kazakhstan and Kyrgyzstan signed a treaty with China and Pakistan regarding cross-border communications. Buses originating in Central Asia can now use this Kaza-Kunlun route to gain direct access to the Indian Ocean. China and Kyrgyzstan and Uzbekistan are preparing to build a railway connecting their three countries and are also constructing the 'East-Line' natural gas pipeline across China to the Pacific coast. This pipeline is regarded by some as the most promising pipeline of the twenty-first century.

Thirdly, from the viewpoint of the economy, economic and trade cooperation will mutually benefit each side. China can provide the Central Asian countries with a great deal of economic and technological assistance. China has had impressive economic achievements in the process of reform and opening up. The Central Asian countries are very interested in China's successful experience in economy especially in terms of structural reform, and the open door policy as it relates to the development of agriculture, fabric production and foreign trade. They hope to strengthen relations with these sectors in China.

Fourthly, China is the biggest country in Asia. China is a permanent member of the UN Security Council that has a population of 1.3 billion and a high rate of economic development. In Asian and what is more in international affairs, China is playing an increasingly important role. Since the Central Asian countries are newly independent countries, developing relations with China will strengthen their status in international life, and will increase their influence, as well as consolidate their political and economic independence. The leaders in the Central Asian countries are stressing that China has an enormous influence on the Third World, as well as on the whole of international society.

Fifthly, since China is a great nuclear power as well as an important force in maintaining peace and security in Asia and the world, in order to protect their national security and to realize domestic and regional stability, the Central Asian countries cannot do without China's help and support.

The cooperation between China and the Central Asian countries in the SCO framework is mainly affected by the following factors:

In the first place, China and Central Asia are closely connected by geography. For China, Central Asia is the door that opens to the European continental land mass while China is Central Asia's most reliable access point to the Pacific. In Chinese terms, the five Central Asian countries are China's friendly neighbors, and the development of a long-standing and stable neighborhood and the development of mutually beneficial relations with these countries is a key element in Chinese foreign policy. Based on the five principles of peaceful coexistence and publicly recognized international relations norms, China hopes continuously to strengthen relations with every Central Asian country. China respects the different paths to development taken by the peoples in Central Asia according to their own national conditions and praises and supports the efforts of each Central Asian country to maintain national independence and regional stability.

Based on equality and mutual benefit, China aspires to expand economic and trade relations with the Central Asian countries; to encourage further and protect mutual investments; to raise the quality of economic and technological cooperation; to make full use of resources and market complementarities; to create new cooperative methods and channels of communication; and to promote mutual development and prosperity. China wishes to strengthen cooperation with the Central Asian countries in communications and transport; to make the most of the 'Euro-Asian Continental Bridge' and the cooperative integration of the various highway systems; to establish perfected mechanisms of cooperation; and to move together to revive the 'silk road'. China wants to strengthen cooperation with the Central Asian countries; to make common efforts towards regional security and stability; to adopt effective methods in attacking the various forms of separatism, terrorism and extremism; and to create a good environment for the continuous development and prosperity of the countries in the region. China is opposed to external forces, especially military blocs that create instability in Central Asia and harm the interests and security of the countries in the region.

Secondly, there is the international factor. China and the Central Asian countries share the status of developing countries. As such they promote new rules and structure, thus they share the same, or similar views on many international issues. China supports multiform, multi-level, multi-track regional security dialogue and cooperation based on equality and consensual negotiation, 'seeking common ground while reserving differences' and gradual orderly progress. China has taken part in some multilateral security dialogues and cooperative processes such as the 'Conference of Asian Mutual Cooperation and Confidence Building'. This format was initiated by the Central Asian countries and China sees in this an important means of fostering cooperation and communications between governments and peoples in the Central Asian non-nuclear area on important security questions. This format will contribute to increased understanding and regional peace and security. Among other Central Asian countries, Kazakhstan considers that Asian countries are becoming increasingly influential in international politics and it is, therefore, important for them to proactively develop their relations with countries in the Asia Pacific region.

China and the Central Asian countries have stressed again and again that they will attack any form of ethnic separatism, religious extremism and international terrorism, and will take action against any organization or force within their own territories that engages in separatist activities and extremist behaviors towards other countries, but they will also oppose attempts to incite religious conflict between states and ethnic groups. They have decided to cooperate in taking severe measures against transnational crimes such as organized crime and the smuggling of weapons. In the region they continue their attacks on the illegal planting, producing and selling of drugs. For these reasons, China and the Central Asian countries are determined to strengthen their regional and international cooperation.

Thirdly, there is the Russian factor. Russia believes that the SCO should become a new international security institution that has geopolitical influence. In 1991, Russia, in terms of its political, ideological and economic relations, 'left' Central Asia. Newly independent Central Asian countries then moved to curtail Russian influence in the region. The Russian-led-regional integration process was not very successful in Central Asia. On the one hand, Moscow attempted to retain its controlling status through the framework established by the collective security treaty of the Commonwealth of Independent States and the Asian European Meeting. On the other hand, the plan for cooperation in the western part of the region does not accord with Russian interests. Russian aid is not predicated in the comprehensive support for the revival of the Central Asian economies. Russia is more interested in consolidating its own security and economic benefits through the SCO. The Russians think that the most dangerous threat will come from the South. They are mainly concerned about how multilateral security cooperation will address anti-Russian sentiment from Chechnya, the exterior Caucasus and Central Asia.

Finally, there is the US factor. As a regional, cooperative and international organization, the SCO is situated far from the US, but, in reality, it cannot escape the dominance of the US. This is because the member countries of the SCO are all developing countries; their economic progress needs technological and financial support from the West, especially from the US; and they all hope to develop mutual, beneficial and cooperative relations with the US. The Central Asian countries of Kazakhstan, Kyrgyzstan, Tajikistan and Uzbekistan are urgently focusing on this. As the world's single superpower, the US has a global strategy to prevent the emergence of a state or bloc of states that can threaten its hegemonic position. Any rising 'opposition' led by Russia or China in an international organization is likely to arouse American concern and worry. Because of this, the SCO and the US will find it difficult to achieve a shared strategic viewpoint with respect to Central Asian sensitivities, or for that matter with respect to the wider international arena. The US may harbor an attitude of distrust towards the SCO, and may even frustrate the SCO in the achievement of its goals.[4] The US military operations in Afghanistan and the US search for a military role in Central Asia, and the many attempts by the Central Asian countries to develop closer military ties with the US, will pose difficult problems for SCO military and security cooperation. The change of Russian policy to the US will also influence the development of the organization. On April 18, 2002, in a state advisory report, President Putin stressed that Russia was prepared to 'participate in the establishment of a new world security system, to keep frequent dialogue with the US and to improve its relationship with NATO'. The two countries are moving closer together with presidential visits. These matters will have indirect influence on the SCO.

On the positive side of this ledger, one might suggest that political, economic and even military pressures from the US will help insure Sino-Russian unity and successful cooperation in the Central Asian region. The Central Asian countries will not completely accept US values. Russia and the Central Asian countries will want to unite with China in a 'balance the power' vis-à-vis the US and this will objectively serve the interests of the 'Organization'. On the other hand, it is not in the American interest to consider the SCO as an enemy, and for this reason, the US will assist the SCO, itself, along with its member countries. Currently, Central Asia is utterly unstable, the Afghan problem has yet to be resolved, the remnants of the Taliban and the 'base' of their organization are still active. The US 'war on terror' is continuing and although the US has support from its Western allies, without the understanding and support of China and Russia it would be extremely difficult for the US to achieve success, especially given the ever-widening frontiers of terrorism. In terms of attacking international terrorism and maintaining regional stability and security, the US and the SCO have no fundamental conflicts. Besides, the cooperative exploitation of resources in Central Asia and the construction of a 'transportation corridor' passing through Central Asia are also in the interest of the US and its allies.

CONCLUSION

Many factors, including history, culture and geography, provide the basis for the development of the relations between China and the Central Asian countries. The dialectical aspects of competing old and new regionalism are complex, but it is argued herein that the increase of Chinese economic power is certainly beneficial to regional cooperation.

The Central Asian countries are very eager to join in the international political and economic system. China can help these countries achieve their objective. The Central Asian countries want to move into Asia, and they want to emulate the economic success of the Asia Pacific economies and in this China can be very useful in helping them realize their goals. Inevitably the Central Asian countries must seek China's help.

China has a very important place in the foreign policies of the Central Asian states, but this position is still not the most important one. Compared with Russia and the US, China has a certain weakness. The Central Asian countries, on the other hand, are not looking for any one country to determine the trend in Central

Asia. Instead, they are hoping that all the exterior powers, including China, can be kept in a balance. Since the SCO includes within its membership two big powers (China and Russia), at the same time it serves as a totally open organization, and it more than satisfies the requirements of the Central Asian countries. The cooperation between China and the Central Asian countries from within the framework of the 'Organization' can help serve regional economic integration and can help solve common security and development problems. This will reflect shared benefit for China and the Central Asian countries, and it will inform the historical trend as they prepare for the broadly-based prosperity that comes with the comprehensive cooperation between China and the Central Asian countries.

NOTES

This article was originally translated from the Chinese by Xu Cai, doctoral candidate in Political Science at the University of Calgary, Alberta, Canada.

1. For discussion of the wider framework of Chinese security initiatives in the Asia Pacific region, see Wang Yushen, 'APEC, ASEM, SCO and [the] New Security Outlook', *Foreign Affairs Journal*, Beijing, No. 64 (June 2002), pp. 71–6.
2. For analysis of China's specific policy perspective on terrorism, see Anti-Terror Research Center, China Institute for International Strategic Studies, 'A Few Observations on Terrorism and Anti-Terror Struggle', *International Strategic Studies*, No. 4 (2002), pp. 18–23. Also for analysis of the Chinese view on the 'three forces' see Pan Guang, 'Xin singshixiade Shanghai hezuo zuzhi: tiaozhan, jiyu he fazhan qianjing' (The Shanghai Cooperation Organization under the New Situation: Challenges, Opportunities and Prospects), *Guoji wenti yanjiu* (International Studies), No. 5 (2002), pp. 38–42.
3. Chinese policy experts like to comment on how the SCO can sponsor a 'new regionalism' that will facilitate a positive relation between the nation-state structure and the global structure of politics. See, for example, Pang Zhongying, 'The Shanghai Cooperation Organization Should Be Built on the Basis of a New Regionalism', *Renmin ribao* (People's Daily), June 24, 2002.
4. There is a variety of American expert opinion on the uses of the SCO; for example, in Charles Morrison and Christopher McNally (ed.), *Asia Pacific Security Outlook, 2002* (Tokyo: Japan Center for International Exchange, 2002), p. 60, and in Charles Morrison (ed.), *Asia Pacific Security Outlook, 2003.* (Tokyo: Japan Center for International Exchange, 2003), p. 50. China's involvement in the SCO and the latter's support for the war on terror are viewed as constructive contributions to regional and global security.

Review Article
Engagement or Confrontation in the Era of Globalization and Democratization

YIJIANG DING

Trade and Human Rights: The Ethical Dimension in U.S.-China Relations by Morris, Susan C. (Aldershot: Ashgate, 2002), 218 pp., £49.00/ $84.95 (cloth), ISBN 0-7546-1837-4.

Inklings of Democracy in China by Ogden, Suzanne (Cambridge, MA: Harvard University Asia Center: Distributed by Harvard University Press, 2002), 430 pp., £31.95 (cloth), ISBN 0-6740-0856-1; £12.95 (paper), ISBN 0-6740-0879-0.

The two books reviewed here deal with apparently very different topics. One is on an American foreign policy issue, the other on China's political development. However, the two authors have essentially raised the same question but provided opposite answers to it. That is, whether the West, especially the US, should encourage the development of democratic values and practices in China through constructive engagement with economic and cultural exchanges and interactions, or through confrontation with moral criticisms and economic sanctions.

TRADE AND HUMAN RIGHTS

Morris offers a focused study of the 1994 decision made by the Clinton Administration to de-link China's Most Favored Nation (MFN) trading status with the issue of human rights in China. The decision marked a major change in American policy towards China. It paved the way for the 1999 US-China agreement on China's entry into the World Trade Organization (WTO), and for granting China the permanent normal trade relations (PNTR) in May 2000. Much of the book is concerned with what motivated the 1994 decision and what political impact it created, especially on human rights as an important issue in contemporary international relations. The 1994 decision is put into the larger context of the relationship between trade and human rights, and between the principle of human rights and the value and principle of national culture and state sovereignty. Three theoretical perspectives – realism, liberalism, and Marxism – are analyzed and found to be valid to a certain extent, but insufficient in providing a comprehensive explanation.

The 'realist' perspective views the 1994 decision as primarily driven by American national interests, namely, US strategic interests in East Asia and its economic interests in the Chinese market. Engagement is considered a better way than confrontation so as to cope with China's growth into a major power, to promote American economic interests in the Chinese market, and to enhance American ability to influence China politically.[1] Realism, however, has its own problems in terms of the difficulty in determining the 'national interest'. Some hardline realists actually supported containment. The realists disagree among themselves on the utility of moral principle in international relations and generally they fail to recognize the 'human dimension'.[2] Some realists challenged the idea of American moral superiority. Others would like to use human rights as 'a manipulative tool' to promote American interests. By the 'human dimension', Morris suggests that since the American people have embraced liberal values, the US government is under pressure to act accordingly. However, one could argue that in 1994, it acted in the national interest, and in spite of the liberal values of the American people.

Liberal perspective saw the 1994 decision as motivated by liberal values. President Clinton justified his 1994 decision by saying that free trade rather than trade sanctions would be more conducive to the promotion of human rights and democracy. Many liberals like to point out that policies of economic liberalization have brought the Chinese people both higher income and more individual freedom.[3] Liberalism, however, is said to have underestimated national interest as a motivation for state actions. Not every country accepts American-style liberal democracy. Promotion of democracy may damage important foreign relations and hurt the US national interest.[4] Many liberals actually opposed the 1994 decision, believing that human rights would suffer as a result. They argued that American foreign policy should be carried out according to American values rather than catering to commercial interests.[5] There is a conflict between the more traditional liberal values such as free market and free trade and the more contemporary liberal emphasis on human rights.

The Marxist perspective explains state actions in terms of capitalist economic interests. Morris points out that, while some big American corporations and business groups lobbied heavily for de-linking trade status from rights and probably influenced the 1994 decision, corporate interests alone cannot adequately explain such a complex policy change. Also, there are different American corporate interests, some of which were actually hurt by the 1994 decision, and lobbied against the renewal of China's MFN status.[6]

Unsatisfied with these conventional perspectives, the author offers a fourth explanation, termed 'complex interdependence', by which she means 'multiple channels of contacts' that form an 'intricate network of transnational actors'. These include transnational corporate linkages, transnational ties among political and business elites, and intergovernmental organizations. National government cannot control these contacts and networks, but are increasingly under their influence.[7]

The distinction between the Marxist perspective and 'transnational corporate linkages' seems a little odd. The author suggests that the latter focus not merely on American corporate interests, but on multinational commercial activities. However, the Marxist perspective also emphasizes 'international capitalism'.

Morris notices that 80 percent of all foreign investment in China comes from small and medium-sized multinational corporations (MNCs) run by overseas Chinese from Hong Kong, Taiwan and Singapore.[8] She suggests that these business interests influence American foreign policy through a 'complex network of regional and global elite alliances'. The latter include prominent political and business leaders in both East Asia and North America. Part of this network is 'a Sino-ASEAN alignment' against 'the post-Cold War international human rights campaign' that is based on authoritarian values. This network of elite alliances is said to have directly influenced the 1994 US decision.[9]

In addition to 'transnational corporate linkages' and 'transnational elite alliances', US foreign policy is also influenced by intergovernmental organizations such as the United Nations (UN), the General Agreement on Tariffs and Trade (GATT)/WTO, the International Monetary Fund (IMF) and the World Bank. The Clinton Administration made the 1994 decision under considerable pressure from these organizations, which, according to Morris, are increasingly coming under Chinese influence as China's economic power grows.[10] The UN's human rights regime is said to have been weakened to the point that it could no longer effectively censure China's human rights violations. The author does not explain how the alleged weakening of the UN's human rights regime influenced the 1994 US decision, other than saying that the free trade agenda has overshadowed the UN's human rights activities.[11] Both the intergovernmental organizations and their free trade agenda might connect with the developing liberal perspective, but the author's analysis does not explore these correlations.

Morris concludes that it was ultimately the external factors, the global trend towards trade liberalization and 'the global concerns for China's integration into the international political economy' that finally persuaded the American government to de-link China's MFN status with its human rights record. To continue the linkage would be acting against a growing international consensus.[12] Rather than recognizing the US as the leading Western power that promotes free trade in the rest of the world, Morris suggests that the international forces of free trade compelled the US to change its position on human rights.

Thus far the book has focused on explaining the 1994 policy change. The analysis has been largely objective and the author's position is only implicitly stated. Her own views, however, become more explicit in her final observations and recommendations. The latter are consistent with a distinctly Western liberal perspective. Non-Western/Chinese perspectives are ignored or criticized. She argues that the 1994 decision indicates a significant weakening of American sovereign power to implement its human rights policy internationally. The assumption appears to be that the US has sovereignty over other countries' human rights. Some of that sovereign power, she claims, has been transferred to multinational corporations and intergovernmental organizations.[13]

To compensate for the alleged weakening of sovereignty, she recommends that the US government pressure MNCs to ensure that they follow human rights principles, that the US pressure the WTO to adopt a 'social clause' to facilitate the imposition of economic sanctions to enforce human rights standards, and that the US continue to pressure China to improve its human rights practices. One wonders how much hostility such external pressures may generate among Chinese people towards the US. She urges American policy-makers to insist on universalism and disregard cultural relativist views of human rights, and to remain focused on the civil and political rights instead of economic, social and cultural rights.[14]

Finally, while she mentions that 'labor standards should not be used for protectionist purposes,' she also calls for the mobilization of the American people – 'the power of consumer sovereignty' – to promote 'socially responsible investment and consumption', and boycott products from countries with human rights violations.[15] There is no discussion of what impact such a mass boycott would produce on the people of other countries, and how they would react to it. A mass boycott of Chinese goods could cause thousands of ordinary Chinese to lose their jobs. In and of itself, this might be construed as a human rights violation. Ordinary Chinese people might in fact question the motives of their 'rights protectors'. Actions taken by human rights activities in developed nations to impose their standards on trade with developing nations have been criticized by developing countries as thinly disguised trade protectionism and economic nationalism – just one more example of Western hypocrisy regarding free trade.[16]

In general, Morris sees the Sino-US trade negotiations as one-way concession-making, with the US making concessions and 'granting' China favorable trading status under various pressures, and compromising American sovereignty in the process. In fact, the process was a two-way street. The granting of MFN status and PNTR was mutual. The Chinese side made considerable concessions in order to gain entry into the WTO. Nicholas R. Lardy's study of China's entry into the WTO reveals that the concessions made by China have allowed the US government to protect some American industries against imports of Chinese goods, even when those goods are fairly traded.[17] Prior to the 1994 decision, the annual congressional review of China's MFN status became a major stimulant of anti-US sentiments in China, where it was generally viewed as American protectionism in the disguise of human rights, and as part of the US effort to slow down China's growth.

Morris raises questions concerning both the cultural differences between the West and China and how the West should approach China on issues concerning human rights and democracy. These questions are the focus of Suzanne Ogden's book on China's political development, in which she deliberately explores the Chinese perspectives on issues of democracy and human rights and the reasons behind those perspectives.

INKLINGS OF DEMOCRACY

Ogden makes two basic claims. First, because of their fundamentally different political culture and tradition, the Chinese understand democracy and human rights very differently from how the Westerners understand those concepts. The Westerners tend to disregard deep-rooted cultural difference as merely an excuse for authoritarianism. Second, as a result of the gradual change in its political culture and institutions in the past 100 years or so, China today has incorporated many Western-style democratic institutions and practices into its political system and is actually democratizing in its own way and according to its own needs, though the outcome of this largely indigenous process may not be a Western-style liberal democracy as many Westerners would like to see.

Ogden argues that different cultures value different sets of rights and have different ideas of justice and good government. The concept of democracy, even the judgment that democracy is good and desirable, is essentially subjective and culturally determined. The Western liberal concept does not represent world-wide consensus.[18] Chinese understanding of democracy is conditioned by its own values and historical experiences. China's traditional culture emphasizes the purpose rather than the form of government, meritocracy rather than democracy, the rule of virtue instead of the rule of law, and social harmony instead of individual rights and freedoms. Confucianism focuses on the proper behavior of the ruler of an authoritarian and paternalist state. Reciprocal moral obligations between the ruler and the ruled form the foundation of social harmony in a hierarchical society.[19]

China's experience with quasi-democratic institutions in the first half of the twentieth century was largely negative, due to the chaos and wars the Chinese people went through. Chinese experience with 'socialist democracy' since 1949 has been more positive, but unlike the Western liberal democracy, 'socialist democracy' has emphasized equality rather than freedom, economic and social rights rather than civil and political rights, a powerful state rather than a limited state.[20] China adopted 'socialist democracy' instead of liberal democracy because of the perceived failures of Western liberalism as demonstrated by the world wars and the Great Depression, the hostility towards Western powers caused by Western imperialism, and mainly because of the preference for a model of modernization that was more compatible with China's traditional culture and historical experience.[21]

In spite of its authoritarianism, Ogden believes that 'inklings of democracy' exist within China's tradition. Such inklings include a degree of cultural pluralism, pantheistic and pluralistic religion, a vibrant market system, a tradition of grassroots autonomy, and a moral justification of people's rights to rebel against tyrannical rulers.[22] 'Inklings of democracy' are also found in the experiments with democracy during the past century, both in institutional forms and in the gradually changing political culture. Ogden suggests that China's current leadership is in fact committed to democratization, but is trying to control the type and the pace of democratization. This attempt to control, she argues, should not be rejected as merely an excuse for keeping the party in power, because it is also out of a concern over social stability and the well-being of the Chinese people.[23] Economic liberalization promoted by the leadership has both benefited the Chinese people economically and severely shaken Chinese society and culture. In this circumstance, caution with the pace of democratization is understandable, because social cohesion is a necessary condition for democratization, while moving too fast 'undermines the very values that have held the society together'.[24]

Ogden believes that democracy cannot be imposed on a society before the society, itself, accepts the idea of democracy. In China, embracing the values of democracy has been an evolutionary process involving incremental and cyclical changes in both political culture and political institutions. The change in each promotes and is promoted by the change in the other.[25] The gap between the West and China in terms of development and democratization should be seen from a historical perspective. Historical stages of development cannot be skipped. The West developed its current democratic system over a long period. China should be allowed to take its time to democratize rather than 'rushed to fit the timetable' set by the West.[26]

Westerners may consider individual freedom a most important value, but most Chinese regard social harmony as more important and associate individual freedom with instability. Westerners cannot assume what is important to them is also desired by others, because what is important is determined by circumstance, experience, and culture. China is faced with the task of providing basic necessities to its large population. Individual freedom would be meaningless if one has nothing else. Ogden's book provides many recent surveys, which reveal that Chinese people are much more concerned with issues concerning their economic well-being, social stability and harmony, clean and effective government, income gap, etc., than with issues concerning individual freedom and political democracy. The government position on the relationship between stability and freedom largely reflects the values of the Chinese people.[27]

The specific meaning of freedom is related to the rights people enjoy in a society. It appears that the Chinese understanding of freedom is more associated with what Ogden terms 'welfare/distributive rights' than with 'civil/procedural rights'. She points out that the two sets of rights do not develop simultaneously and may even be in conflict with each other. In fact, Western democracies have largely abandoned the idea of absolute freedom that some Westerners try to impose on China. Freedom is now understood more positively as the capability to achieve well-being and to develop human potential. This meaning of freedom justifies the Chinese focus on welfare/distributive rights.[28] Ogden contends that the Chinese people have gained a lot of rights since 1949, including the rights to security, adequate nutrition, health care, education, employment, housing, etc. Women's rights increased tremendously between 1949 and 1979. Since the beginning of economic liberalization in 1979, individual rights and freedoms have increased significantly, including the rights to choose jobs, place to live, consumer goods, and personal life style, and the rights to privacy, free speech and access to information.

Ogden believes that individual rights and freedoms are to a certain extent gained at the cost of the welfare/distributive rights that the Chinese people gained before the economic liberalization. The right to choose one's job has replaced the right to job security. Emphasis on economic efficiency leads to the abandoning of the housing assignment system – a decrease in urban residents' right to housing. In poor rural areas, people's rights to health care and education have also decreased. The revival of traditional attitude has negatively affected women's rights.[29] Social order and stability has deteriorated, due to a growing income gap, the revival of criminal gangs, and the reduced ability of the state to control society. The trade-off between individual rights and welfare/distributive rights has been justified by the need for fast economic development and by the fact that most people in China have benefited from economic liberalization.[30]

Ogden thinks that the Chinese leadership remains committed to reforms that will allow the Chinese people to enjoy more rights and freedoms. In addition to economic liberalization, limited political reforms are introduced. People's congresses are strengthened at all levels, and are directly elected at the township and county levels.[31] The National People's Congress (NPC) is becoming increasingly powerful. Within the state sector, the selection of officials now involves soliciting the opinion of employees through polls. The party has formally endorsed the idea of the 'rule of law' and the principle of judicial independence. A large number of laws have been made to protect people's rights. Although the enforcement has lagged significantly behind, putting the laws on the books is considered a necessary first step towards legal protection of rights.[32]

Chinese sources testify to the increasing number of lawsuits in recent years and attributes such increase to the Chinese people's growing awareness of their rights, their growing willingness to use law to protect their rights, and the availability of law for rights protection. A recent report shows the number of lawsuits brought by individuals against government administrative units increased from about 27,000 in the year 1992 to over 100,000 in 2002. Cases that were won increased from 22 percent to 26 percent. Cases that were lost decreased from 36 percent to 29 percent. Cases that were withdrawn decreased from 38 percent to 32 percent.[33]

The policies of economic liberalization have led to the creation of thousands of associations – a Chinese style 'civil society'. Though many associations are used by the government to impose a degree of control over their memberships, they become increasingly autonomous in their pursuit of membership interests, and behave more and more like interest groups in their relationship with government. Some have become important forces in shaping government policies. The large number of associations has offered Chinese citizens a wide range of opportunities to participate in public life. Associations have become an important way for people to pursue their special interests.[34]

In view of China's achievements, Ogden believes that most Chinese would probably prefer that the Chinese Communist Party (CCP) remain in power. The political dissidents attempting to overthrow the CCP do not offer a viable alternative. To overthrow the CCP may destabilize China and jeopardize economic growth, a risk most Chinese are not willing to take. The CCP is a product of China's authoritarian political culture, but it is also ruling over a people in whom the same political values are deeply embedded.[35] The party has now incorporated different factions representing a broad spectrum of social interests. The reformers that control the party initiated economic liberalization, abandoned the idea of 'class struggle', and moved the party rightward to the political centre. The triumph of the recent theory of 'three representatives' confirmed that the hardline Leninists have been marginalized. In a democratizing China, the CCP may well become the mainstream party in a one-party dominant system, following an East Asian model of democratization, as exemplified by the Liberal Democratic Party in Japan and the Nationalist Party in Taiwan.[36]

Ogden concludes that China today is an authoritarian system that is gradually democratizing. Basic democratic institutions – 'the trappings of democracy' – are already present. What is needed is for them to continue to evolve along the current trajectories. 'They have, in fact, already evolved to a point where they are far more democratic than at any time in Chinese history.' [37] She suggests using an 'internal critique' and a utilitarian perspective to evaluate the political progress in China, which is to judge a society by its own standards of what is just, fair and democratic. Cross-national surveys indicate that the Chinese are more satisfied with life and more optimistic for the future than the world average.[38] Using the 'human development index' adopted by the UN, Ogden finds that China has done better than most developing countries.[39]

Ogden's message is clear. The West should stop trying to impose its own values and models on China. Her book is highly informative and extremely thought-provoking. It raises fundamental questions about the purposes of government and how they can be achieved in different cultural contexts. She challenges the view that the Western-style liberal democracy is the only form of government that is able to provide its citizens with good life and justice. She argues that each society has its own priorities based on its own value orientations. The meaning of democracy as an ongoing process varies from culture to culture, since the two basic values of democracy – freedom and equality – are fundamentally incompatible with each other. Each society that is democratizing must find its own balance that is suitable for its own culture.[40]

A COMPARISON OF THE TWO AUTHORS

Thus, the two authors reviewed here present the readers with opposing views on a number of issues concerning the political and cultural relationships between the West and China and how Chinese cultural and political development is to be understood and evaluated. Morris and Ogden take contrasting positions in their cultural perspectives, their understanding of 'rights', their assessment of China's political development, and their recommendations concerning how the West should approach China on the issue of human rights.

Cultural Perspectives

Morris adopts a Western-centered universalist perspective. She clearly takes the view that human rights transcend cultural boundaries and are absolute and universal. Her recommendation to US policy makers is to 'develop and maintain a nonrelative position towards international human rights'. She argues that 'the notion that rights are subject to the interpretation of cultures is a detriment to the betterment of human rights around the world'. Specifically regarding China, she condemns the use of 'Asian culture' as an excuse for a different approach to the development of human rights.[41]

Ogden, on the other hand, defends a qualified cultural relativist position, which she defines as the sensitive understanding of the culturally determined rationale behind preferences made by people of other cultures. She writes:

> ... relativists reject the notion that one can objectively judge other people's values and actions as inferior. To do so is merely an effort to assert one's own superiority. Relativists recognize that upbringing, culture, history, and even songs, foods, and customs affect who people become.[42]

Her own book is a good example of putting herself in someone else's shoes, not in order to adopt other people's views, but in order to understand why other people do things the way they do, what are their standards, and what is the rationale that underlies their standards. Applying this position to ideas of freedom, democracy, and human rights, she contends that there has never been a universal standard applicable to all places at all times.[43]

Understanding 'Human Right'

The opposition in the two authors' cultural perspectives is connected with, and illustrated by, their different understandings of the substance of human rights. Morris adopts the Western liberal position that focuses on civil and political rights instead of economic, social and cultural rights. She suggests that the focus on economic, social and cultural rights has been made an excuse for lack of development of civil and political rights, and rejects as invalid 'the view of a duality between civil and political rights and economic, social and cultural rights'.[44]

Ogden disagrees. She contends that 'procedural rights', which emphasize civil and political justice, are often at odds with 'distributive rights', which includes the basic economic and social rights. Procedural rights seek freedom. Distributive rights seek equality. The two values are fundamentally incompatible with each other. For an obvious example, the principle of individual freedom simply contradicts the idea that everyone has the right to be employed. One conclusion of her book is that the development of procedural rights in China in recent years has been at some cost to people's distributive rights. People want freedom and democracy, she argues, not for its own sake, but in order to have a good life and justice. Distributive rights are primary human rights because they bring people a good life and are crucial to the development of human capacity. China is justified to give priority to distributive rights in order to meet its own developmental needs and as a necessary step towards a just society.[45]

Evaluation of China's Human Rights Situation

Given the sharply different cultural perspectives and ideas of human rights, the two authors naturally disagree on how China's human rights situation should be evaluated. Morris is negative. She sees little improvement in human rights in China. Citing reports from sources such as Amnesty International, the US State Department, and the US Congress, she paints a bleak picture of China's human rights.[46] Ogden, on the other hand, offers a detailed analysis of the rights gained by the Chinese people since the CCP came to power in 1949, especially since the economic reforms began in 1979 and concludes that the Chinese people today enjoy far more rights than they have ever done in the past. This difference may originate in Ogden's profound knowledge of China's past and present, and her ability to look at the present situation from a historical perspective.[47]

The adoption, or the lack, of a historical perspective leads to opposing views on the pace of the country's political development. Morris is impatient with China's apparent slow pace, despite the progress made in economic liberalization.[48] Ogden, on the contrary, is on the whole satisfied with the current pace of China's political development and optimistic about its future. She believes that 'China is moving at a fair pace' towards democratization. She even suggests that 'it could be easily argued that the pace of democratization in China is not too slow, but too fast, and hence too destabilizing for the long-term health of society'.[49] The two authors also disagree on what motivates the improvement of human rights in China. Morris sees international pressure as the primary motivation, and suggests the need to use economic sanctions and boycotts to pressure China to improve its human rights.[50] Ogden regards domestic cultural and social changes as the primary motivation, and is obviously in favor of engagement with China through cultural and economic interactions.

The disagreement on evaluation is partially due to the different sources of information the two authors rely on. Morris relies on reports made by Western human rights groups, the US State Department and the US Congress. One Amnesty International report cited by Morris claims that 'the 1.2 billion people cannot speak out...' [51] The assumption seems to be that the 1.2 billion Chinese are all anti-government. They do not speak out because they are all silenced by the government. Ogden, on the hand, has done much fieldwork in China, herself, and relies heavily on Chinese scholarly sources for her assessment of China's political development. She questions the accuracy and objectiveness of the sources used by Morris. For example, the sources cited by Morris condemn China's criminal justice system for much of China's human rights abuses. Ogden argues that China's criminal justice system has been treated 'quite incorrectly' by Western human rights groups, which ignore the significant progress China has made in recent years in improving its legal system, including its criminal justice system, and in offering Chinese people greater legal protection of their rights, including the rights of the accused and the rights of the prisoners. Western human rights groups, according to Ogden, have also failed to understand 'the strength of popular support' for actions taken by China's criminal justice system.[52]

A case in point is the large number of death penalties carried out in China each year. Amnesty International, cited by Morris, reported 1,067 executions in China in the year 1998 alone.[53] However, Chinese people by and large support the government's harsh measures against criminal activities and the execution of those whose crimes they believe to be very serious. In other words, actions taken by China's criminal justice system largely reflects the political values of the Chinese population. Ogden carefully points out that 'popular support for state actions that violates human rights does not excuse the state's behavior'. However, it helps explain why there is not much criticism against such repression from Chinese people, themselves.[54]

Ogden accuses the Western powers of using double standards: 'They judge themselves and their allies differently from the way they judge China.' [55] Her own standard of evaluation combines the indigenous perspective – how the Chinese themselves feel about their situation, with a utilitarian perspective, which emphasizes rights that bring people good life and social justice.

CONCLUSION

On balance, Morris is strong in her analysis of what motivated the American government's decision to de-link trade and human rights, but rather weak in her argument in favor of a Western universalist perspective that justifies greater external pressure as the primary means to improve human rights in China. In my opinion, the position taken by Morris is problematic. On an issue of monumental importance like human rights in China, one simply cannot ignore the Chinese views. Though it is not her intention, Morris's own analysis reveals that the human rights issue has been raised against China not simply out of a genuine moral concern for Chinese people's rights, but for a host of other reasons, including concerns for US hegemony in the face of rising Chinese power, American trade protectionism, etc.

Ogden, on the other hand, has offered compelling and convincing evidence to support her view that the ideals of democracy and human rights are taking root in China, but largely on the basis of Chinese understandings, and mainly as a result of domestic economic, social, cultural and political changes. This view of China's political development justifies constructive engagement as a much more effective way in facilitating democratization. A confrontational approach with high-handed moral criticisms and efforts to impose Western models is counter-productive. The choice between the two approaches is, in the final analysis, a matter of cultural tolerance. A balance between universalism and cultural tolerance is necessary in the development of common values. Such a balance services 'cultural globalization'. This does not entail any necessary reduction of basic human values. It simply means to allow people of different cultures to realize those values in their own ways through their own historical development. Ogden may have overemphasized the tenacity of traditional authoritarian political values, but she carefully points out that Chinese culture is evolving and many elements of Western culture, including some important Western liberal democratic values, are gradually being accepted.[56]

Those who feel that constructive engagement has not delivered democratization in China need to have a better understanding of what is happening in China today. Instead of focusing solely on some repressive actions of the regime, it is necessary to have a wider and longer view, take note of the profound changes in Chinese society, and have a little more patience. Tradition weighs heavily in China and political change takes time. Transition to democracy took over a century in the West. Similar transition in China, which started nearly a century ago, is likely to take another generation to complete. While this historical process is being played out, engagement – promotion of economic and cultural interactions – is far more preferable than confrontation in the relationship between the West and China.

NOTES

1. Susan C. Morris, *Trade and Human Rights: The Ethical Dimension in U.S.-China Relations* (Aldershot: Ashgate, 2002), pp.75–78.
2. Ibid., pp. 18–20, 73–5.
3. Ibid., pp. 87, 89–90.
4. Ibid., pp. 25–6.
5. Ibid., pp. 91–2.
6. Ibid., pp. 93–4, p. 97.
7. Ibid., p. 109.
8. Ibid., pp. 111, 124.
9. Ibid., pp. 122–3, 127.
10. Ibid., pp. 116–9. China's contribution to IMF, hence its voting power, has increased significantly in recent years. A recent book by Supachai Panitchpakdi, Director-general of WTO, describes China as an engine of regional growth. See Supachai Panitchpakdi and Mark L. Clifford, *China and the WTO* (Singapore: John Wiley & Sons [Asia] Pte Ltd., 2002), pp. 115–7.
11. Morris, *Trade and Human Rights*, p. 120.
12. Ibid., pp.128, 140.
13. Ibid., p. 149.
14. Ibid., pp.154–9. A Chinese perspective on human rights always emphasizes national conditions and developmental needs and focuses on economic, social and cultural rights rather than civil and political rights. As Panitchpakdi and Clifford point out, China has been quite successful in providing its people with basic needs and lifting millions of Chinese out of poverty. See Panitchpakdi and Clifford, *China and the WTO*, p. 154.
15. Morris, *Trade and Human Rights*, pp. 157, 159–60.
16. See Panitchpakdi and Clifford, *China and the WTO*, pp. 61–2.
17. See Nicholas R. Lardy, *Integrating China into the Global Economy* (Washington DC: Brookings Institution Press, 2002), pp. 85–8, 104.
18. Suzanne Ogden, *Inklings of Democracy in China* (Cambridge, MA: Harvard University Asia Center: Distributed by Harvard University Press, 2002), pp. 14–6.
19. Ibid., pp. 21, 41–6. Kevin O'Brien's study of 'grassroots democracy' in China reveals that democratic development in rural China is saddled with traditional values. The peasants' notion of their rights is associated with the traditional view of the relationship between the ruler and the ruled as one of reciprocal obligations. See Kevin O'Brien, 'Villagers, Elections, and Citizenship,' in Merle Goldman and Elizabeth J. Perry, *Changing Meanings of Citizenship in Modern China* (Cambridge, MA: Harvard University Press, 2002), pp. 212–31.
20. Ogden, *Inklings of Democracy in China*, pp. 19–21.
21. Ibid., pp. 74–8.
22. Ibid., p. 52.
23. Ibid., p. 82.
24. Ibid., p. 91.
25. Ibid., pp. 83–5.

26. Ibid., pp. 95–6.
27. Ibid., 121–4. The same conclusion is reached by Thomas Lum in his study on the obstacles to democratization in China. He finds that the Chinese people give the highest priority to social stability and economic well-being. See Thomas Lum, *Problems of Democratization in China* (New York: Garland Publishing, Inc., 2000), p. 69.
28. Ogden, *Inklings of Democracy in China*, pp. 125, 130.
29. This is confirmed by a recent study on Chinese women by Margaret Woo. See Margaret Woo, 'Law and the Gendered Citizen', in Goldman and Perry, *Changing Meanings of Citizenship in Modern China*, pp. 308–29.
30. Ogden, *Inklings of Democracy in China*, pp. 138–41.
31. A study by Young Nam Cho confirms that China's local people's congresses have become an increasingly independent power in local politics. See Young Nam Cho, 'From 'Rubber Stamps' to 'Iron Stamps': The Emergence of Chinese Local People's Congresses as Supervisory Powerhouses', *The China Quarterly*, Vol. 171 (Sept. 2002), pp. 724–40. Michael W. Dowdle's study shows that the NPC is becoming increasingly assertive in exercising its power. See Michael W. Dowdle, 'Constructing Citizenship: The NPC as Catalyst for Political Participation,' in Goldman and Perry, *Changing Meanings of Citizenship in Modern China*, pp. 330–52.
32. Ogden, *Inklings of Democracy in China*, p. 244.
33. See Tian Yu, 'Jin 50 wan jian 'min gao guan' yiwei zhe shenmo?' (What is the Significance of Nearly Half a Million Cases of 'People Suing Government'?) *Remin Ribao* (People's Daily), Feb. 15, 2003, p. 2. See also Gao Hongjun, 'Zhongguo gongmin quanli yishi de yanjin' (Evolution of the Consciousness of Citizen's Rights in China), in Xia Yong *et al.*, *Zouxiang Quanli de Shidai* (Towards the Era of Rights) (Beijing: Chinese University of Politics and Law Press, 1995), pp. 32–8.
34. Ogden, *Inklings of Democracy in China*, pp. 291–300, 316. A recent article by Bruce Dickson also noticed an emerging of organized interest groups among China's private entrepreneurs, who use their associations to press for group interests. See Bruce Dickson, 'Do Good Businessmen Make Good Citizens?' in Goldman and Perry, *Changing Meanings of Citizenship in Modern China*, pp. 255–87.
35. Ogden, *Inklings of Democracy in China*, pp. 180–81. Thomas Lum suggests that most intellectuals in China who are critical of the regime are in fact 'loyal dissidents' who advocate gradual political change from above, to avoid social instability and disruptions to economic development. See Lum, *Problems of Democratization in China*, pp. 128–9.
36. Ogden, *Inklings of Democracy in China*, pp. 97, 261–2, 313–4. The theory of 'three representatives' gives prominence to business people and the intellectuals. The CCP subsequently revised its constitution to allow private entrepreneurs – the bourgeoisie – to join the party. Bruce Dickson points out that the CCP is now increasingly a party of new economic and intellectual elites. See Bruce J. Dickson, 'Political Instability at the Middle and Lower Levels', in David Shambaugh, *Is China Unstable?* (Armonk, NY: M.E. Sharpe, 2000), pp. 40–56.
37. Ogden, *Inklings of Democracy in China*, p. 354.
38. Ibid., pp. 357–61.
39. Ibid., p. 371.
40. Ogden's position that Western countries are faced with the same problem of balance between freedom and equality is supported by John Rawl, the political philosopher whose principles of justice aimed at such a balance.
41. Morris, *Trade and Human Rights: The Ethical Dimension in U.S.-China Relations*, pp. 154–5.
42. Ogden, *Inklings of Democracy in China*, p. 24.
43. Ibid., pp. 24, 362.
44. Morris, *Trade and Human Rights*, p. 155.
45. Ogden, *Inklings of Democracy in China*, pp. 363–5.
46. Morris, *Trade and Human Rights*, pp. 2, 142–5.
47. People with knowledge of history tend to take a historical view of the current development. Another example is found in H. Lyman Miller, 'How Do We Know If China Is Unstable?' in Shambaugh, *Is China Unstable?* pp. 18–25.
48. Morris, *Trade and Human Rights*, p. 144.
49. Ogden, *Inklings of Democracy in China*, pp. 6, 379. The 'liberals' among China's intellectuals may disagree. They have adopted the view that democratization needs to keep pace with economic and social development in order to avoid a 'participation crisis'. See Yijiang Ding, *Chinese Democracy after Tiananmen* (Vancouver: UBC Press, 2001), pp.26–7.
50. Morris, *Trade and Human Rights*, pp. 159–60.

51. Ibid., p. 2.
52. Ogden, *Inklings of Democracy in China*, p. 231.
53. Morris, *Trade and Human Rights*, p. 2.
54. Ogden, *Inklings of Democracy in China*, p. 231.
55. Ibid. p. 363.
56. Barrett McCormick, though regarding China as moving a little too slowly towards democracy, has expressed a similar view by saying that the Western scholars debating on the pace of China's political reform generally 'agree that China has already taken important steps towards democracy'. See Edward Friedman and Barrett McCormick (eds), *What If China Doesn't Democratize?* (Armonk, NY: M.E. Sharpe, 2000), pp. 4, 339.

INDEX

For Product Safety Concerns and Information please contact our EU
representative GPSR@taylorandfrancis.com
Taylor & Francis Verlag GmbH, Kaufingerstraße 24, 80331 München, Germany